SADLIER'S
Coming to Faith Program

COMING TO
GOD

Dr. Gerard F. Baumbach

Dr. Eleanor Ann Brownell

Moya Gullage

Joan B. Collins

Helen Hemmer, I. H. M.

Gloria Hutchinson

Dr. Norman F. Josaitis

Rev. Michael J. Lanning, O. F. M.

Dr. Marie Murphy

Karen Ryan

Joseph F. Sweeney

Patricia Andrews

The Ad Hoc Committee
to Oversee the Use of the Catechism,
National Conference of Catholic Bishops,
has found this catechetical text to be
in conformity with the
Catechism of the Catholic Church.

with

Dr. Thomas H. Groome
Boston College

Official Theological Consultant
   The Most Rev. Edward K. Braxton, Ph. D., S. T. D.

Scriptural Consultant
   Rev. Donald Senior, C. P., Ph. D., S. T. D.

Catechetical and Liturgical Consultants
   Dr. Gerard F. Baumbach
   Dr. Eleanor Ann Brownell

Pastoral Consultants
   Rev. Msgr. John F. Barry
   Rev. Virgilio P. Elizondo, Ph. D., S. T. D.

Catechetical Assessment Consultant
   Dr. George Elford

William H. Sadlier, Inc.
9 Pine Street
New York, New York 10005-1002

D1406531

Nihil Obstat
✠ Most Reverend George O. Wirz
Censor Librorum

Imprimatur
✠ Most Reverend William H. Bullock
Bishop of Madison
May 9, 1997

The *Nihil Obstat* and *Imprimatur* are official declarations that a book or pamphlet is free of doctrinal or moral error. No implication is contained therein that those who have granted the *Nihil Obstat* and *Imprimatur* agree with the contents, opinions, or statements expressed.

Printed in the United States of America.
Credits appear on page 288.

Home Office:
9 Pine Street
New York, NY 10005-1002

ISBN: 0-8215-4301-6
78910/030201

DEAR GIRLS AND BOYS,

Coming to God is your book. It has been written especially for you. Your religion book will help you to come to know and love God more and more.

In your **Coming to God** book you will find wonderful things to think about, to talk about, to do and to learn by heart. You will find:

- stories about boys and girls who love God just as you do;
- prayers to help you listen and talk to God;
- stories from the Bible, especially about Jesus, God's own Son;
- the story of our Catholic Church;
- action prayers to help you celebrate God's love for you and all people.

All of these things can help you to grow in your love for God and other people. We hope you will have a wonderful time this year as you come closer to God. During the year be sure to share what you learn and think and feel with your family.

All of Us in the Sadlier Family

Contents

Unit 1   God Gives Us the World   page

Doctrine: Catholic Teaching

Unit 1 Review and Unit 1 Test —see pages 255 and 256

Unit 2	God Gives Us Jesus	page

Doctrine: Catholic Teaching

Unit 2 Review and Unit 2 Test—see pages 257 and 258

First Semester Review and First Semester Test — see pages 259 and 260

Unit 3   Jesus Christ Gives Us the Church   page

Doctrine: Catholic Teaching

Doctrine: Catholic Teaching

Gather together in a circle.
Join hands.
Now pray together.

✝ Thank You, God, for bringing us together.

Leader: Dear God, help us to learn about You.
All: We love You, God.

Leader: Dear God, help us to love You.
All: We love You, God.

Leader: Dear God, help us to be like You.
All: We love You, God.

Leader: Dear God, help us to pray to You.
All: We love You, God.

Together sing the song
on page 9.

Here We Are, God!

OUR LIFE

God, help us to learn about You together.

Let's take turns. Tell everyone your name.
Share your own special hello with us.

SHARING LIFE

Sing this coming together song.
(To the tune of "Did You Ever See?")

♫ Oh, we all have come together
Together, together.
Oh, we all have come together
To learn about God.

We're happy to be here.
We'll all help each other.
Oh, we all have come together
To learn about God. ♫

How do you feel to be learning about God?

9

OUR CATHOLIC FAITH

God wants us to learn
many things this year.
We will learn many wonderful
things about God together.

We can help one another
listen and learn about God's love.

We can share our Catholic faith
as we read and listen to stories
from the Bible.

We can share our faith by drawing,
singing, and praying together.

We can help one
another to live
our faith.

11

COMING TO FAITH

Look at your *Coming to God* book.
Is there something you want
to learn about God this year?
Take turns telling a friend about it.

PRACTICING FAITH

Put your hands flat on the floor.
Pray,
† God, we know that You are with us.

Join hands with your friends
beside you.
Pray,
† God, help us to learn together
many wonderful things about You.

Hold your right hand over your heart.
Pray,
† God, help us to listen and learn
about Your wonderful love.

Take a few minutes to point out the
"Faith Alive" sections to the children.
Encourage them to share the activities with their families at a special
time each day.

12

REVIEW

Look at the children on page 12.
Draw yourself showing one way
you like to pray.

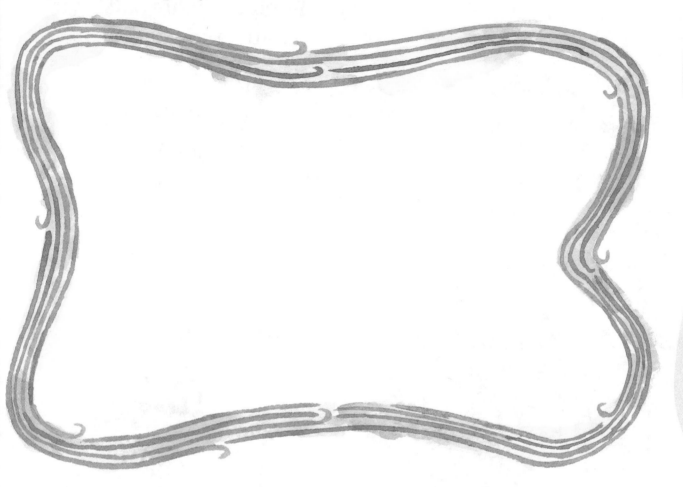

FAITH ALIVE AT HOME AND IN THE PARISH

This year your child's program in learning our Catholic faith is called *Coming to God*. You have already spent time preparing your child for this continuing growth of coming to God. You have, informally and gently, been teaching your child about God and about God's love all along. Now you can take an even more active role in guiding your child's growth in faith this year.

Learn by heart

Faith Summary

- We help one another learn about God's love.

- We share our Catholic faith.

1 God Made the World

OUR LIFE

Do you like to discover things in the world?
Imagine you are outside in your favorite place.

Look up.
What do you discover?

Look all around.
What do you discover?

Look down.
What do you discover?

Name some more of your favorite things in our world.

SHARING LIFE

Why is our world so wonderful?

Do you know who made it?

Let's think about God's wonderful world.
Look at each picture on these pages.

Tell what time of year it is.
How do you know?

What is it like where you live in summer?
in autumn? in winter? in spring?

Why did God give us our wonderful world?

This week we will discover many
more things about our world.

We Will Learn

- God the Father made
  the world.

- He made the animals.

- He made everything good.

Let's pray our opening prayer
again to tell God how we feel
about our wonderful world.

15

■ Thank You, Father, for our wonderful world!

■ Who put the stars in the sky? Who made the sunshine?

God Made the World

Everything good comes from God.

This is His story of creation from the Bible.

Read to me from the Bible

God made the sun, the moon, and the stars.
The light helps us to see.
The light makes us warm.
God said, "It is good."
From Genesis 1:3–4

God made the water.
The water is good to drink.
The water makes plants grow.
God said, "It is good."
From Genesis 1:9

God made the earth.
God made the plants, trees, and flowers.
God said, "It is good."
From Genesis 1:10–13

Name something that is good to drink.
Name something that smells good.
Thank God for making our world.

Who made the world?

How will you thank God the Father
for our world?

OUR CATHOLIC FAITH

■ O God, everything You made is good.

■ Why did God make so many good things?

God Made the Animals

God made all living things in our world. God made so many wonderful animals!

Big animals were made by God. Horses, lions, and elephants were made by Him, too.

Name some big animals. Show how they move.

Little animals were made by God. Ants, kittens, and puppies were made by God.

Name some little animals.
Show how they move.

The animals are God's gift to us.
They are our helpers and friends.
God wants us to be kind to
animals.

- To what animal can you
  be kind?

- Close your eyes. Thank God
  in your heart for your favorite
  animals.

OUR CATHOLIC FAITH

God our Father, help us to be kind to animals.

Why did God make all the good things in our world?

God Made Everything
Creation is everything made by God.
All of creation is His gift to us.

All God's creation is good!
We can know God through the things God made for us.
God is the creator of all things.

We can praise and thank God for all the wonderful things in creation.

Praising God's Creation

Saint Francis loved everything in God's creation.

This is the way Saint Francis praised and thanked God for creation.

✝ Be praised, O God, for Brother Sun.
  He gives us your light.

Be praised, O God, for Sister Moon.
  She brightens the night.

Be praised, O God, for Brother Wind.
  He brings all kinds of weather.

Be praised, O God, for Sister Water.
  She is cool and refreshing.

Add your own prayer to praise God for something you love in the world.

Learn by heart **Faith Summary**

● God made everything.

● All God's creation is good.

21

COMING TO FAITH

Sing this song about God's
wonderful world.
(To the tune of "The Farmer in the Dell")

♫ The birds fly in the sky.
The fish live in the sea.
We all live in a wonderful world
God made for you and me. ♫

Can you tell or act out how you
feel about God's wonderful world?

PRACTICING FAITH

Finish this prayer with a picture.
I thank You, God, for _____

Take turns praying your picture
prayers.
Then pray together,
† Thank You, God, for all creation.

22

Take a few minutes to go over the
"Faith Alive" section with the children. Encourage them to share with
you the song they learned in
this chapter.

REVIEW ▪ TEST

Circle **Yes** or **No**.
If you are not sure, circle **?**.

1. Creation is everything made
by God.   **Yes**   **No**   **?**

2. People made the animals.   **Yes**   **No**   **?**

3. All God's creation is good.   **Yes**   **No**   **?**

4. Everything good comes from God. **Yes**   **No**   **?**

5. Draw one wonderful
thing God made.

FAITH ALIVE AT HOME AND IN THE PARISH

In this lesson your child learned about God the creator and the wonderful world that is God's gift to us. Talk to your child about the beauty of God's world and ways to appreciate and enjoy it. Then do the following activities together.

Creation Song

Have your child sing for you the song he or she learned on page 22. Together make up another verse for the song.

Creation Posters

Have fun finding pictures of wonderful things in God's world. Help your child cut them out and paste them on a large sheet of paper. Let your child choose and write a slogan for the poster. Hang the poster in your child's room or some prominent place in your home.

2 | God Made People

Our Life

Look at me!
I am wonderfully made!
I have
eyes for seeing,
ears for hearing,
a nose for smelling,
a mouth for tasting and talking,
and hands for touching, hugging,
and holding.

Sharing Life

Act out one wonderful thing you can do.
Why can you do so many
wonderful things?
Who gave you so many gifts?

Choose one gift God has given you. Think of all the things you can do with this gift.

Now look at the pictures on this page. Tell how you use your gift at home, in school, in church, and at play.

Tell God in your heart how you feel about having this gift.
What would it be like if you did not have this gift?
Share your ideas with a friend.

In this lesson we will discover how wonderful we are because God made us.

We Will Learn

- God our Father made people.
- He made us wonderful.
- We are to be like God.

- Thank You, God, for all Your gifts to us.
- Why does God love all people?

God Made People

Everything God made is good.
God made people.
People are very special to Him.

Here is a story from the Bible.

Read to me from the Bible

God said, "Let Us make people.
They will be like Us."
So God made people.
God made a man and a woman.
God said, "Both men and women are very good."
From Genesis 1:26–31

God made all kinds of people.
He made big people and small people.

God made people with dark skin.
He made people with light skin.

No two people are exactly alike.

All people are beautiful because
God made us.
We are God's children.
He loves us all.
We are to love one another.

✝ Thank You, God, for all kinds of people.

Who made people?

Why are all people so special?

OUR CATHOLIC FAITH

Loving God, help us to love all people.

What special things can you do?

God Made You

Before you were born,
God called you by name.
He said, "What a wonderful person

_____

- -

_____

will be!"

God gave you your eyes for seeing,
your ears for hearing,
your nose for smelling,
your mouth for talking and tasting,
and your hands for feeling and
holding and hugging.

How wonderfully made
you are!

Create means God making something new.

God made you.
God loves you.
He loves every part of you.
God is our loving creator.

Color and pray.
† God, You created me.

I AM

wonderfully made.

From Psalm 139

■ Who made you so wonderful? Why?

■ How will you thank God for making you so wonderful?

29

■ Make up a thank you prayer to thank God for your eyes, ears, nose, mouth, and hands.

■ Share your prayer with a friend.

You Are Like God

God knows and loves and creates.
He made you to know and love
and make things, too.

A teddy bear is a wonderful thing.
But a teddy bear cannot know things.
You can know many things.
God made you to know and learn.

A teddy bear cannot love.
A teddy bear cannot give you a hug.
You can hug. You can love.
God made you to love everyone.

A teddy bear cannot draw.
You can draw. You can make music.
You can make many new things.

You can know and love and
make things.
You are to be like God.

We Are Caretakers!

God wants you to use the wonderful gifts you have.
God wants you to take care of yourself and other people!

Look at the pictures.
Name ways to take care of yourself.
Name ways to take care of others.
What other ways can you think of to use the gifts God gave you?

Learn by heart **Faith Summary**

- God made me wonderful.

- I can know, love, and make things.

31

Coming To Faith

Choose a partner. Act out ways you can know, love, and make things. See if your friends can tell what you are doing.
Who made you able to do all these wonderful things?

Practicing Faith

Let us thank God for making people so wonderful.

Gather in two celebration circles. The inside circle moves to the left. The outside circle moves to the right. Stop at each friend and shake hands. Say, "God made you wonderful!" Do this until you have celebrated each person.

Talk to the children about what they and their families might do on the "Faith Alive" section. Encourage them to find a family member who will do the Sharing Gifts activity with them.

REVIEW ▪ TEST

Circle **Yes** or **No**.
If you are not sure, circle **?**.

1. God knows, loves, and creates.   **Yes**   **No**   **?**

2. God made only me wonderful.   **Yes**   **No**   **?**

3. God made and loves all people.   **Yes**   **No**   **?**

4. We are to be like God.   **Yes**   **No**   **?**

5. How does it feel to know that God
loves you? Show it on this face.

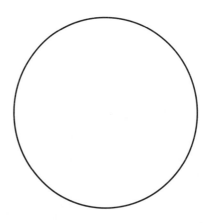

3   God Gives Us Life

God, I am so happy to be alive!

OUR LIFE

What would it be like
if nothing made sounds?

What sounds do lions make?
Can you make these sounds? Do it.

How would you feel
if nothing could move?

How do dolphins move?
Can you move like them? Do it.

SHARING LIFE

What can a flower do
that a rock cannot do?

What can a lion do
that a flower cannot do?

What can you do that a flower
and a lion cannot do? Why?

34

Celebrate being alive.
Make up actions for this poem.

Read to me
Flowers can grow,
Lions can roar,
Frogs can leap,
Birds can soar.

I can think
And learn each day.
I can love
And laugh and pray.

Life is super,
Life is great,
Life is something
To celebrate.

Are you glad to be alive?
Show it! Shout, "Hooray for life!
Thank You, God, for the gift of life!"

In this lesson we will learn about
the life of God that is in us.

We Will Learn

- God gives us the gift of life.

- God gives us the gift of human life.

- God gives us His own life.

35

Praise God for all living things.

Who gives us the gift of life?

God Gives Us Life

When God made the world,
He made living things, too.
The Bible story tells us what God
told all living things to do.

Read to me from the Bible

God told all the fish in the water to
fill the sea, all the birds in the air to
fill the sky, and all the animals on
the land to fill the earth.
From Genesis 1:20–24

What a wonderful gift life is!
Imagine all that living things can do.

Living things can move.
Living things can fly.
There are living things that grow.
There are living things that crawl
and walk and make sounds.

There are living things
all over the world.
Living things are gifts from God.

† Thank You, God,
for all living things.

Who gives the gift of life?

How will you thank God today
for the gift of life?

OUR CATHOLIC FAITH

Thank You, God, for the gift of life.

What is good about being alive?

The Gift of Human Life

All life is a gift from God.
God gives plants, animals, and all living things the gift of life.

Of all the things God made,
He loves people most.
People are more important than plants and animals.
People have human life.

Human life is a gift from God.
Human life is always special.
Human life is very precious to God.
God gives us the gift of human life through our parents.

Grace is God's own life and love in us.

God wants us to care for all living things. He wants us to care especially for human life.

Who cares for you? Is there someone you help care for?

Draw a picture of yourself caring for a living thing.

Why is human life always special?

Share your pictures. Talk about whom or what you are caring for.

39

Praise God. God's love for us is strong.

Why do you think God made you?

God's Own Life

God is a loving Father.
We are God's children.
God gives us His own life.
We call God's life in us grace.

Grace is a special gift we have from God. It is God's own life and love in us.

You have God's grace.
You can say, "God is my loving Father.
I am God's own child."

Our Protectors

Your life is very precious to God.
Like a loving mother or father,
God protects your life.
God often uses other people to do this.

Look at the pictures.
Name the different people
you see. Tell how they protect you.

Draw a picture of another person
who protects you.
What will you say to that person
the next time you meet?

Learn by heart **Faith Summary**

- God gives us the gift
  of human life.

- Grace is God's own life
  and love in us.

41

Coming To Faith

What do you want to say to God about the gift of life?

Celebrate God's gifts of life and grace in you.
Join your friends in a circle.
Make up actions to go with the song.
(To the tune of "Are You Sleeping?")

♫ Who has God's life?
We have God's life.
Yes we do! Yes we do!
Thank You, God, for Your life.
Thank You, God, for Your grace.
We love You. We love You. ♫

Practicing Faith

Life is very precious.
What will you do today
to take care of
the gift of life?

† Let us pray together,
Thank you, God, for giving
us Your gifts of life and love.

Take a few minutes to discuss with the children the "Faith Alive" section. Encourage the children to do the Child of God activity with a family member.

REVIEW ■ TEST

Circle **Yes** or **No**.
If you are not sure, circle **?**.

1. Of all living things, God loves
plants most.   **Yes   No   ?**

2. Human life is our gift from God.   **Yes   No   ?**

3. God gives us human life through
our parents.   **Yes   No   ?**

4. I am God's own child.   **Yes   No   ?**

5. Tell what we call God's own life
and love in us.

4   God Knows and Loves Us

Loving God,
how much You
love each of us.

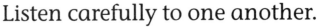

OUR LIFE

Let's get to know our friends better.
Talk with a partner about some
favorite things,
    a favorite toy,
    a favorite thing to do outside,
    a favorite thing to do on a rainy day.
Listen carefully to one another.

Do you think you know
each other better now?

SHARING LIFE

How does knowing people
help us love them better?

Do you think God wants us to love
one another? Why?

Sit in a friendship circle.
Take turns telling what you
learned about your partner.

Talk together about what you
can do to be good friends.
Draw a picture of one way you
can be a good friend inside this space.

✝Loving God, help us to be friends.

In this lesson we will discover how
much God loves all people and
wants us to be friends.

We Will Learn

- God knows and loves us.

- People need other people.

- God wants us to care for the world.

45

■ Loving God, thank You for loving us so much.

■ Tell something you know about God.

God Knows and Loves Us

God knows and loves us.
He made us out of love.
We are called God's children.

From 1 John 3:1

God always loves and cares for us.
God's love is a gift.
God's love for us will never end.
God wants us to love one another.

There is only one God.
There are three Persons in one God,
God the Father, God the Son,
and God the Holy Spirit.

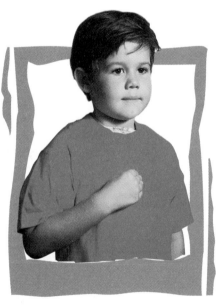

In the name
of the Father,

and of the Son,

We call the three Persons in one God
the Blessed Trinity.

The Sign of the Cross

When we begin our prayers to God,
we say,

✝In the name of the Father,
and of the Son,
and of the Holy Spirit. Amen.

We call this the Sign of the Cross.
This prayer can always remind us
of God's great love for us.

- Make the sign of the cross now.
- Will you say this prayer before
  you go to bed tonight?

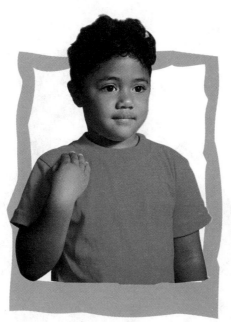

and of the Holy   Spirit.   Amen.

OUR CATHOLIC FAITH

- We pray in the name of the Father, and of the Son, and of the Holy Spirit. Amen.

- Why do we need other people?

We Need People

There are people all over the world.
Think how many.
Some people are near us.
Other people are far away.

People need other people.
A goldfish can live alone in a bowl.
A canary is happy by itself.
But God made people
to be friends.

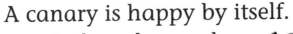

God wants us to care for one another.
We care for people when they are sad or when they are lonely.
We care for people when they are afraid.

God loves us like a loving father or mother.
God wants us to love others as our sisters and brothers.

How can we care for people?

For whom will you care?

Jesus, bless our world.
Help us to keep it beautiful.

Tell how you care for it
and why.

Our Beautiful World

We are part of the wonderful
world God made.
God our Father gives us our
beautiful world.
He wants us to take care of
and enjoy our world.

We plant seeds.
We sail on the sea.
We can fly through space.

Each of us can do something
to keep our world beautiful.

Making the Sign of the Cross

Catholics make the sign of the cross when we begin and end our prayers.

We make the sign of the cross with holy water when we go into church.

When the priest blesses us at the end of Mass, we make the sign of the cross again.

Every time we make the sign of the cross, we should think of what we are saying.

Let's make the sign of the cross together now.

Learn by heart **Faith Summary**

- God knows and loves us.

- God made us to love one another.

Coming To Faith

To show that you are God's child, whisper your name where you see the heart.

God made ♥ and others out of love.

God always loves and cares for ♥ and others.

God wants ♥ and others to love one another.

God loves you so much. How does this make you feel?

Practicing Faith

Think of some people in your parish who show you that God loves you. How will you thank them?

Let us make the sign of the cross together as our closing prayer.

Talk to the children about the "Faith Alive" section. Encourage them to show someone at home how they can make the sign of the cross.

REVIEW ∎ TEST

Circle **Yes** or **No**.
If you are not sure, circle **?**.

1. There is only one God.   **Yes**   **No**   **?**

2. There are three Persons in one God.   **Yes**   **No**   **?**

3. The Blessed Trinity is three Persons
in one God.   **Yes**   **No**   **?**

4. God's love for us will end.   **Yes**   **No**   **?**

5. Show how you make the sign
of the cross.

FAITH ALIVE AT HOME AND IN THE PARISH

This week your child learned to make the sign of the cross, a sign of blessing and of our belief in the triune God. God the Father, God the Son, and God the Holy Spirit are each fully and eternally God. Yet our faith is always in one God, a unity of three in one. The mystery of the Blessed Trinity is the central mystery of Christian faith and life. God has revealed to us this mystery of faith. The doctrine of the Blessed Trinity helps us to understand that God is our Creator, Redeemer, and Sanctifier. Catholics begin worship and prayer in the name of the Trinity by making the sign of the cross.

The Sign of the Cross
Invite your child to show how he or she can make the sign of the cross. Pray it together before your child goes to bed.

We Care
Ask your child to think of ways that your family can care for our world. Choose one of them that you will do together this week. Perhaps you can invite other families in the parish to join with you in this work of caring.

5 God's Promise

OUR LIFE

Read to me
A promise is a special thing
I say that I will do.
The reason that it's special is
I give my word to you.

A promise can be broken, but
I hope that mine won't be.
I want to be the kind of friend
Who keeps my word, you see.

Who are your friends?
Do you make promises to them?
Do you ever break your promises
to them?

What does it mean to keep a
promise?

SHARING LIFE

Choose a friendship partner.
Tell each other how it feels
to have a friend
who keeps promises.

Why should we
keep our promises?

Finish this story with your friendship partner.

Read to me

When the Ortiz family adopted a kitten, Juan and Maria promised to take care of it. One day their father asked them to help clean the litter box. Juan and Maria both made a face and said, "Yuck!"

What do you think Juan and Maria should do?
Tell why it is sometimes hard to keep a promise.

In this lesson we will discover that God always keeps promises.

We Will Learn

- God promises to love us always.

- Adam and Eve turned away from God.

- God keeps God's promise to us.

- God, help us to be like You. Help us to keep our promises.

- What promises do you find it hard to keep?

God's Promise

God promises to be with us and to love us always.
Here is a Bible story that helps us remember God's promise of love.

Read to me from the Bible

The first man and woman lived in a beautiful garden called Eden. Their names were Adam and Eve. God promised they would be happy always if they did what God asked. They had everything they needed. But they still wanted more.

From Genesis 2:8—3:6

God asked Adam and Eve
to choose. They could love
or not love Him. God wanted
them to choose what was right.

God wants us to choose what
is right. He wants us to live
as God's children. We can
choose to love or not love God.
We can love or not love
one another.

- What does God promise us?
- What do you choose to do?

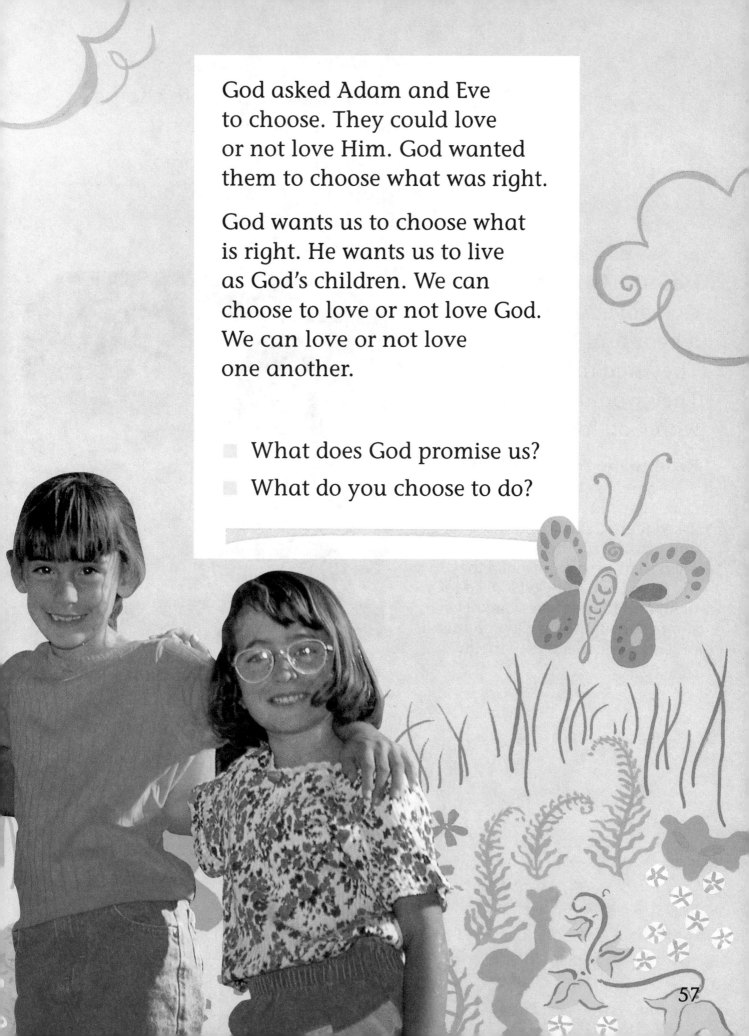

OUR
CATHOLIC
FAITH

■ Loving God, help me to choose what is right and to do it.

■ How do you feel when you do something you should not have done? Why?

People Turn from God

God gave Adam and Eve a beautiful home.
They had all they needed.
They would be happy with God forever.

Read to me from the Bible

Adam and Eve turned away from God. They did not do what God asked them to do. This hurt Adam and Eve and all their children. Then they felt ashamed. So they hid from Him. But God looked for them and found them. God never stopped loving them. God promised to send Someone to help them.

From Genesis 3:6–15

We are the children of Adam and Eve, too.
Sometimes we do what we should not do.
But God never stops loving us,
no matter what we do.
He wants us to be sorry and do our best.
God loves and cares for us always.
We can be happy with Him forever.

Write one word to tell how you feel
because God loves you.

_____

- -

_____

Share your word with a friend.

- Can you thank God for
  always loving you? How?
- Will you thank Him?

OUR CATHOLIC FAITH

Jesus, help us to love as God loves us.

How can you show you love God?

God Keeps the Promise

When Adam and Eve said no to God, they did what was wrong.
But God did not leave them alone.
He promised to help them and their children.

God kept this promise by sending us Jesus, His own Son.
Jesus shows us how to love God.

Jesus shows us how to love one another.
If we live as Jesus shows us, we can be happy with God forever.

† Thank You, God,
for keeping Your promise.

Good Listeners

God speaks to us in many ways.
He wants us to be listeners—really
good listeners.
How can you be a good listener?

One way is to be very still,
very quiet with God.
God will be with you.

You can be very still, too, at Mass
when God's stories are read.
You can pay attention to the stories.
You can tell them to others.

You can be a good listener in your
religion class.
Listen as your teacher tells you
about God.
Listen to what your friends say
about Him, too.

What kind of a listener will you be
this year?

 Learn by heart **Faith Summary**

- People turned away from God.

- God promised to save us and
gave us Jesus, God's own Son.

COMING TO FAITH

What does God promise us?

Sit quietly and pray in your heart.
Think about God's promise.
Hold your right hand over your heart.
Tell God how you feel.
† Then say, "God, thank You
for loving me so much.
I will always love You."

PRACTICING FAITH

A rainbow is a sign to us
of God's promise of love.
Make a group "rainbow promise
banner." Put on your banner,
"God always loves us."

Hang your banner in the church
or parish center.
Invite the people at your church to
sign their names on your banner.
† Together pray, "Thank You, God,
for promising to love us always."

God Always loves us

Invite the children to share their faith
at home this week. Encourage them to
tell their families about the "rainbow
banner" and to invite their families to
come and sign it.

REVIEW ■ TEST

Circle **Yes** or **No**.
If you are not sure, circle **?**.

1. Adam and Eve obeyed God.   **Yes**   **No**   **?**

2. God broke God's promise to us.   **Yes**   **No**   **?**

3. Sometimes we do what we
should not do.   **Yes**   **No**   **?**

4. God will love us always.   **Yes**   **No**   **?**

5. God sent someone to show us how
to love God and others. Who was it?

_____

- -

_____

FAITH ALIVE ■ AT HOME AND IN THE PARISH

This week your child learned the biblical story of the creation of the first human beings. The story is not intended as a literal account of a historical event; it tells us, however, that God is our creator and that human beings lost the original gift of God´s friendship. We call this original sin. The story also reminds us of the reality of sin in our world and in our lives. Because of the very gift of freedom that God gave to us, we are able to turn from God—we commit sin.

However, God did not abandon the human race. God promised to send a Savior: "The Lord will give you a sign: a young woman is with child and will have a son whom she will call 'Immanuel'" (from Isaiah 7:14). Immanuel means "God is with us."

Promises to Keep

Talk together about promises and ways we should try to keep them. Sometimes it is hard to keep a promise, but God will always help us. God always keeps God's promise to love us.

Then pray together:

✝ Thank You, God, for loving us always. Help us to keep our promises.

6 The Bible

God, open our
ears and hearts
to listen
to Your word.

Our Life

Leader: Let us gather and quietly listen to very important words from the Bible, the book that is God's gift to us.

Reader: God says, "Be very quiet and listen to Me! Do not be afraid— I am with you!"

From Isaiah 41:1,10

All: God, listening to Your word makes us happy!

Reader: Jesus says, "Happy are those who do what God wants. He will bless them fully."

From Matthew 5:6

Sharing Life

How do you feel when you hear God say, "Do not be afraid—I am with you."? Tell about it.

Trace this bookmark on a sheet of paper.

Cut it out and decorate it.

Go over the words in your favorite color.

Write your name on the back.

Then put it in your religion book as a marker.

This year we will be hearing and reading many of God's stories from the Bible.

When you hear a story that makes you feel happy and close to God, ask your teacher to help you find the story in your class Bible. Then put a bookmark in the Bible so you can always find your favorite story.

We Will Learn
- The Bible is God's story.
- The Bible tells us about God and God's love for us.

A long time ago some people wanted
to tell God's story. They began by thinking
about who made the world. They thought
about who made them.

God helped the people to find answers
to their questions. They wrote the story
of all that God had done for them. We call
God's story the Bible.

The stories in the Bible tell us about
God and His love for us. We listen to
God's story often, and we learn about
His gifts to us.

The Bible tells us about God's best gift.
God's best gift is Jesus Christ,
His own son.

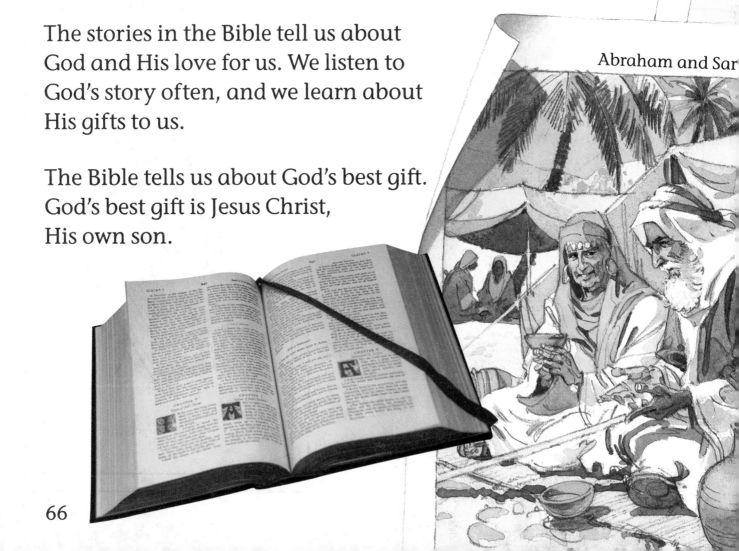

Abraham and Sar

Ruth

Palm Sunday

Coming To Faith

Let us share this song to tell God that we want to be good listeners to His word.
(To the tune of "If You're Happy")

♪ Oh, God, we're happy listening to Your word.
Oh, God, we're happy listening to Your word.
Oh, God, we give You glory
As we listen to Your story.
Oh, God, we're happy listening
to Your word. ♪

Practicing Faith

Make a "Happy Listener" badge. Wear this badge when you listen to God's story in the Bible.

Wear your badge now as we carry the Bible to a special place.

Leader: Let us sing "Oh, God, We're Happy Listening to Your Word."

Leader: Let us pray with actions. Follow the pictures.

† **All:** God, listening to Your word makes us happy.

God, keeping Your word makes us happy.

God, sharing Your word makes us happy.

Talk with the children about ways they and their families might use the "Faith Alive" section. Encourage them to share the prayer on their badges with their families.

REVIEW ▪ TEST

Circle the correct answer.

1. The Bible is God's _____.

    life   story   world

2. We listen to God's _____.

    music   letter   message

3. God's best gift to us is God's own _____.

    Son   Sunday   prayer

4. Tell a favorite story from the Bible.

FAITH ALIVE AT HOME AND IN THE PARISH

In this lesson your child was introduced to the Bible, the word of God to us written in human language. It is the book that every Catholic should read, reflect on, and love. The Church urges us to pray and meditate on the Bible as a primary source of spiritual growth and wisdom for daily life.

Learn by heart

Faith Summary

- The Bible tells about God and His love for us.

- We listen carefully to God's message.

O God, we honor
all Your saints
today.

OUR LIFE

Read to me

All the children in the
neighborhood like Mr. Gorski. He
tells them stories and fixes their
broken toys. He lets them play in
his yard. He always talks with them
when they come to visit.

The children and their families
want to honor Mr. Gorski in a
special way. They are planning a
neighborhood party for him. The
day will be known as "Mr. Gorski's
Special Day."

Imagine you live in Mr. Gorski's
neighborhood. What would you
do for the party?

SHARING LIFE

Who is a special person you
would like to honor? Why?

How would you show that you
honor this person?

70

Fill in this "honor poem" and show it to the person you would like to honor.

Dear _____,
You are so good,
Here's how I'd honor you
If I could.

If I were a
I'd sing, sing, sing!
If I were a
I'd ring, ring, ring!
If I were a
I'd fly up high!
If I were a
I'd wave in the sky!

But I am me—what can I do?
I'll say what I feel—I love you!

This week we will learn why the Church honors people called saints.

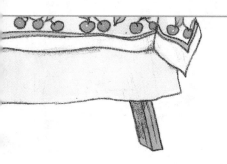

We Will Learn

- Saints loved God and did His will.
- We honor all the saints on a special day.

OUR CATHOLIC FAITH

In our Church we honor some special people each year on November 1. These special people are called saints.

Saints are people who love God and others very much. They did what God wanted them to do during their life on earth. Now they are happy with Him forever in heaven.

When they were alive, the saints tried to do the things Jesus told us to do,
• feed the hungry,
• help poor people,
• pray to God each day,
• share their things with others,
• be kind and fair to everyone,
• be peacemakers.

We do not know the names of all the saints who are with God in heaven. We celebrate the feast of All Saints to remember and honor all these special people.

Coming To Faith

Form two lines and face each other.
(Sing to the tune of "Do You Know the Muffin Man?")

♫**Group 1**

Do you know Saint Elizabeth,
Saint Elizabeth, Saint Elizabeth?
Do you know Saint Elizabeth?
She fed the poor and hungry.

Group 2

Yes, we know Saint Elizabeth,
Saint Elizabeth, Saint Elizabeth.
Yes, we know Saint Elizabeth.
Saint Elizabeth, pray for us.♫

Add to your song. Use these words
to honor these saints.

Saint Joseph
He cared for Jesus and Mary.

Saint Thérèse
She did little things for Jesus.

Saint Martin
He helped the sick and homeless.

Saint Nicholas
He helped the needy children.

PRACTICING FAITH

How will you be like the saints?
How will you honor the saints
on November 1, All Saints' Day?
The pictures can help you decide.

Cut out the saints' cards on page 281.
Pray the prayer printed on the back.
Draw one of your favorite
saints on the empty card.
Share your cards with your
family and friends.

Talk with the children
about ways they and
their families might use
the "Faith Alive" section.
Encourage them to share
their saints' cards with
their families.

REVIEW ▪ TEST

Circle the correct answer.

1. On November 1, the Church honors _____.

        all people   the saints

2. November 1 is called the feast of _____.

        All Saints   Christmas

3. Saints try to live as _____ taught them.

        their friends   Jesus

4. Saints are people who _____ God and others.

        save   love

5. Tell one thing you can do to become a saint.

FAITH ALIVE ▪ AT HOME AND IN THE PARISH

This lesson deepened your child's understanding of what it means to be a saint. A saint is someone recognized by the Church for living a holy life. The early Christians used this word to include all those who have done or are doing God's will. A saint, then, is someone who truly lives the gospel teachings of Christ. The Second Vatican Council reminds us that all Christians are called by Baptism to such holiness of life.

Learn by heart

Faith Summary

- Saints are people who loved God and did God's will on earth.

- We celebrate the feast of All Saints on November 1.

8 The Story of Jesus

Our Life

Everyone was so happy
the day you were born!
Everyone said, "What a beautiful baby!

Welcome, _____."
(your name)

What do you know about the day
you were born?
Tell your story.

Sharing Life

Why are people happy when
a new baby is born?

Pretend you are talking
to Jesus when He was born.
What would you say?

With your friends, make a welcome blanket to celebrate Jesus' birth.

Trace one of these shapes on a paper square. Decorate the square. On it, print a message to Jesus. Join all the squares together. Take turns praying your messages.

Tell something you already know and like about Jesus.

In this lesson we will discover more wonderful news about Jesus.

We Will Learn
- Jesus is God's own Son.
- Jesus is one of us.
- Jesus is part of our human family.

OUR CATHOLIC FAITH

- Pray together some of the messages to Jesus you wrote on page 77.

- Tell what you know about the birth of Jesus.

The Story of Jesus

God wanted to give us the gift of Jesus. Jesus is His own Son. God asked Mary to be the mother of Jesus. Mary said yes to God.

From Luke 1:26–38

Mary always did what God asked.

Read to me from the Bible

Mary was married to Joseph. They went to a town called Bethlehem. There was no room for them at the inn. So they had to stay in a stable. There Mary gave birth to Jesus, God's own Son. Mary laid Jesus in a manger.

From Luke 2:4–7

We celebrate Jesus' birth at Christmas.

At **Christmas** we celebrate the birth of Jesus.

Act out the Christmas story with your friends.

How will you thank God for Jesus?

79

OUR CATHOLIC FAITH

■ Lord Jesus, You are God's greatest gift.

■ Do you think Jesus was like you? How?

Jesus Was One of Us

Do you think Jesus laughed and played and sang?
Do you think Jesus ever felt afraid or alone?
Do you think Jesus ever got tired?

Think of the things you love to do.
Jesus did some of them, too.
He was one of us. Jesus laughed and played with His friends.
He loved and shared with them.
Sometimes He felt afraid or got tired as we do.
Jesus is one of us.

Jesus learned how to read.
He studied the Bible.
Mary and Joseph taught Him to love and pray and work.
We call Jesus, Mary, and Joseph the Holy Family.

80

Jesus, Mary, and Joseph did the things that families do together. They tried to love one another every day.

Imagine being with Jesus, Mary, and Joseph.
What are they like?

Draw the Holy Family at home.

■ With a friend, explain how Jesus is like us.

■ Jesus, Mary, and Joseph, help our families to be full of love.

OUR CATHOLIC FAITH

- Whisper this prayer very slowly: Jesus...Mary...Joseph...be with us today.

- Tell some things you do to help your family.

Jesus and Our Family

There are many kinds of families. Some families are big, others are small. Some families have two parents, and others have one. Some families live together, others do not.

Family members try to love one another.
They want the best for one another.
Jesus, God's own Son, wants the best for us, too.

Today Jesus is still part of our human family.
Jesus helps our families to love and care for one another as He did.

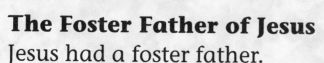

The Foster Father of Jesus

Jesus had a foster father.
He was Jesus' special protector.
We call him Saint Joseph.

Even before Jesus was born, Joseph loved and took care of Mary. Then Joseph loved Jesus and cared for Him. Joseph taught Jesus how to be a carpenter. He also helped Jesus to pray and read the Bible.

Think about someone who loves and protects you.

Draw pictures of some of the things these people do for you.

Ask Saint Joseph to care for those who protect you.

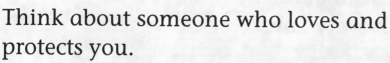 **Faith Summary**

- Jesus is God's own Son.

- Jesus is one of us.

Coming To Faith

Imagine you are going to visit
the Holy Family for the whole day.
What might you do together?
What might you say to one another?
How would you feel?

Practicing Faith

Pray in your heart. Ask Jesus, Mary,
and Joseph to help your family be a
holy family.

Color the prayer banner. Share the prayer
with your family. Invite your family to
write their names on it. Put your banner
where your family will see it every day
this week.

Holy Family
be with our family. Amen.

84

Take a few minutes to
go over the "Faith
Alive" section with your
children. Encourage
them to tell the
Christmas story to
someone at home.

REVIEW ■ TEST

Fill in the circle beside the correct answer.

1. We celebrate the birth of Jesus on _____ .
   ◯ Easter   ◯ Christmas   ◯ Thanksgiving

2. The foster father and protector of Jesus is _____ .
   ◯ John   ◯ Joseph   ◯ Jesus Christ

3. The mother of Jesus is _____ .
   ◯ Anne   ◯ Elizabeth   ◯ Mary

4. Jesus, Mary, and Joseph are the Holy _____ .
   ◯ Trinity   ◯ Church   ◯ Family

5. Tell how Jesus was like us.

FAITH ALIVE AT HOME AND IN THE PARISH

This week your child learned that Jesus is both the Son of God and the son of Mary. He is true God and true man in the unity of His divine Person. Because Jesus was human like us, He shared the same joys and sorrows we share. He was one of us; as Scripture reminds us, He was "like us in all things but sin" (Hebrews 4:15). This affirmation of the full humanity and full divinity of Jesus Christ is a central dogma of our faith.

A Holy Family

Help your child to understand that Jesus was born into a human family. Jesus, Mary, and Joseph are called the "Holy Family." They really loved and cared for one another. Make a list together of ways your family can try to be holy. Then pray:

† Jesus,
Help us to be like you
In what we do and do not do.
Help us to be loving and kind.

Mary and Joseph, pray for us
to be a holy family.

9 Jesus Is God's Own Son

Our Life

Read to me

Yesterday was my dad's birthday. I wanted to show him how much I love him. But I had no money to buy him a gift.

Then I remembered a special rock I had in my treasure box. Dad and I found it on our walk one day. I rubbed the rock with oil to make it shine. I gave it to my dad at dinner.

After dinner Dad told me, "Your gift was my favorite. It really showed your love."

Name some things you treasure.

When would you ever give your treasure as a gift?

Sharing Life

Can love be a gift? Why?

Why is love the best gift of all?

What are some of the best gifts God gives us?

Everyone can give the gift of love. Act out ways you can give love as a gift.

Trace and decorate this rock. Cut it out and write your name on it. Wear it to remind you to give the gift of love today.

In this lesson we will discover more about Jesus, God's best gift of love to us.

We Will Learn

- Jesus did things only God can do.
- Jesus shows us that God loves us.

GIVES

- Dear God, thank You for the gift of Your love.

- What kind of gift does not come in a box?

Jesus is God's Own Son

God gives us many gifts. His greatest gift to us is Jesus Christ, His own Son.

Read to me from the Bible

One day when Jesus was grown, His cousin John saw Him walking by the Jordan River. John told people to get ready for Someone special.

Then John baptized Jesus in the river. God the Father spoke from heaven and said to Jesus, "You are My own dear Son. I am pleased with You."

From Mark 1:9–11

Jesus traveled from place to place telling people about God's love. He helped people who needed Him.

Jesus showed people how much God loved them.
He showed them how to love and care for one another.
He taught them to care for poor people in a special way.

What Jesus did and said showed that He was the Son of God.

- Explain why Jesus is God's greatest gift to us.

- Be very still. Quietly thank God for giving us Jesus.

■ Jesus, help us learn what You will teach us today.

■ Tell some ways that Jesus showed He was God's own Son.

Jesus Is God

Jesus showed people how to love God.
Jesus showed them how to love one another.
Jesus did things only God could do.

Read to me from the Bible

One day, Jesus and His friends were in a boat. Suddenly a strong wind began to blow. The waves began to fill the boat. Jesus' friends were afraid.

Jesus stood up and told the wind and the sea, "Be quiet!" At once, the wind stopped blowing. The sea was quiet.

The friends of Jesus said, "Who can this be that the wind and the sea obey him?"

From Mark 4:35–41

Jesus' friends knew that only God could stop a storm at sea.

Write
Jesus is the

~~Son of God.~~

- How do you know that Jesus is the Son of God?

- What will you do to show Jesus you love Him?

OUR CATHOLIC FAITH

■ Jesus, help us to know You.

■ What do you know about Jesus?

Jesus Shows Us God

Jesus is one of us, and Jesus is God.
People could see Jesus.
They could touch Him.
They could hear Him and look at His face.

People may ask us, "What is God like?" We can say that Jesus showed us in many ways what God is like.

He showed us by what He did and said.

Jesus said, "Anyone who has seen Me has seen the Father."

From John 14:9

Jesus showed us that God is love. Tell something that Jesus did that shows us what God our Father is like.

The Name of Jesus

The name of Jesus is very holy.
We use it only with respect.
Catholics often bow their heads
when they hear or say His name.
We do this to show love and
respect for the holy name of Jesus.

Here is a prayer to Jesus.
Pray it together.
When you say Jesus' name,
bow your head.

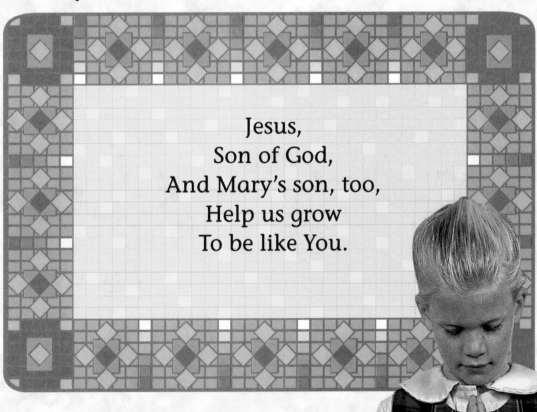

Jesus,
Son of God,
And Mary's son, too,
Help us grow
To be like You.

Learn by heart **Faith Summary**

- Jesus is God's greatest gift to us.

- Jesus shows us He is God's own Son.

COMING TO FAITH

Sometimes the captain of a boat has
something important to tell.
First the captain says on the
loud speaker, "Now hear this!"

Take turns being the boat captain.
Say, "Now hear this!"
Then tell everyone something Jesus
did or said to show us what God is like.

PRACTICING FAITH

Have a "Now hear this!" parade.
Sing this song as you march.
(To the tune of "Mary Had a Little Lamb")

♫ Jesus is God's gift to us,
Gift to us, gift to us!
Jesus is God's gift to us.
He is God's own Son.

Jesus shows God's love for us,
Love for us, love for us!
Jesus shows God's love for us,
He is God's own Son. ♫

Can you teach this song to someone
at home?

"Now Hear This!"

For the children's participation in the
"Faith Alive" activities, encourage
them to teach their new song to
someone at home.

REVIEW ■ TEST

Circle the correct answer.

1. Jesus Christ is _____.

   the Son of God   the Holy Spirit

2. God's greatest gift to us is _____.

   Jesus   the Church

3. What Jesus did and said showed
   that He was _____.

   the Father   the Son of God

4. Tell the story of something Jesus did that
   shows who He is.

FAITH ALIVE AT HOME AND IN THE PARISH

Your child learned this week that Jesus Christ is God's best gift to us. He is the second Person of the Blessed Trinity who came into the world to fulfill God's plan of salvation. Jesus became one of us and shared our human condition. He was like us in everything but sin. By His life, death, and resurrection, Jesus brought new life to all humankind. Jesus is our Savior and Redeemer.

† Prayer of Thanks

Read this passage from Scripture to your child: "God so loved the world that God sent God's own Son to give us eternal life."
From John 3:16

Share some of your own thoughts and feelings about Jesus and invite your child to do the same. Then pray together thanking God for the gift of Jesus.

10 Jesus Is Our Friend

Jesus, help us
to live as
Your friends.

Our Life

Read to me
I want to draw a picture of
The best friend there could be.
Here's what I'll put in the picture.
I hope you will agree.

A great big heart for loving,
And eyes to look and see;
I'll draw two ears for listening,
To be like you and me.

I'll add two hands for helping,
A mouth for smiling, too.
Now count the many special things
That your best friend can do!

Do you have a best friend?
What do you like to do together?

Sharing Life

Jesus wants to be your best friend.
How does that make you feel?

How can you be a good friend to Jesus?

Your thumbprint is special. No one else has a print just like yours.

Make a thumbprint picture of yourself. Write your name under the picture.

We are all different, but we are all friends of Jesus. Tell why you are a friend of Jesus.

In this lesson we will discover more about Jesus Christ, our best friend.

We Will Learn
- Jesus loves and cares for all people.
- Jesus healed people.
- We pray to Jesus our friend.

Jesus, help us to be Your good friends.

Explain why you think Jesus is your good friend.

Jesus Is Our Friend

Jesus loved and cared for everyone.
He hugged little children.
He healed people who were sick.
He helped people who were sad
or afraid.
He cared especially for poor people.
Jesus cared for people who were not
easy to love.
He was fair to everyone.
He even loved those who hated Him.

Jesus said: "Love your enemies.
Do good to those who hate you."

From Luke 6:27

Jesus is the best friend we can have.

Sometimes we are sick or sad.
Sometimes we feel alone or afraid.
But we are never really alone.
Jesus is always with us.
He loves and cares for us.
Jesus is always our best friend.

Color and pray.
Thank You, God, for giving us

JESUS.

What do you learn from the things Jesus did for people?

Why is Jesus always our best friend?

OUR CATHOLIC FAITH

- Jesus, help us to believe in You.
- Share a favorite story about Jesus.

Jesus Healed the Sick
Sick people came to Jesus.
They believed in Him.
They asked Him to make them well again.
When Jesus touched them, they got better.
Jesus healed them.
Jesus healed all their hurts.

Read to me from the Bible
One day, some people brought a deaf man to Jesus. They asked Jesus to help the deaf man. Jesus touched the man's ears and said, "Be opened!" All at once, the man could hear. Then the man gave praise and thanks to God.
From Mark 7:32–35

Can you imagine how the man felt!

Prayer is talking and listening to God.

Many people believed in Jesus.
They came to Him for help.
Jesus made them well.
Jesus cared for people who were sick, sad, or unhappy.

Jesus wants all of us to be healthy.
He wants everyone to be happy.

Draw someone Jesus helped.
Tell about it.

- What did Jesus do for people who came to Him for help?

- How and when will you ask Jesus for help?

OUR CATHOLIC FAITH

Jesus, we always need Your help.

How did Jesus help people in need?

We Can Pray to Jesus

Prayer is talking and listening to God.

We can always talk or pray to Jesus.
We can tell Jesus we love Him.
We can thank Him for being our best friend.

We can ask Jesus to help us and others.
If we do things that are wrong, we can tell Jesus we are sorry.
Jesus always forgives us.

We can pray anywhere, anytime.
We can pray in the morning, at night, or before we eat.

Jesus always hears our prayers.

Praying for Others

Do you know that you can help other people by your prayers? We can ask God to comfort or heal someone.

Praying for others is like giving them a special gift.

God always hears our prayers for others. He answers them in a way that is best for each person.

Work together to make cards for people in your parish who need your prayers. Pray together for each person by name.

Learn by heart **Faith Summary**

- Jesus cares for all people.

- We can pray to Jesus our friend.

COMING TO FAITH

Pray this new way.
Imagine that you are sitting
on Jesus' lap.
Tell Jesus what you like best
about being His friend.

PRACTICING FAITH

Here is a prayer song to sing.
(To the tune of "Playmate")

♫ Jesus, my best friend,
Oh, You are always there.
You show me how to share,
You show me how to care.
Oh, You're my best friend,
I've learned what friends
    are for —
To love and share and care
Forever more! ♫

Now look at the pictures on
this page. Circle the ones
that show when you will pray
to Jesus.

Take time to go over the "Faith Alive"
activities with the children. Talk about
setting up a "prayer corner" at home.
Pray together the prayer on page 99.

104

REVIEW ▪ TEST

Circle the correct answer.

1. When we talk and listen to God we _____.

    work   pray   study

2. Jesus _____ people who were sick.

    left alone   healed   talked about

3. When we are sorry, Jesus _____ forgives us.

    always   sometimes   never

4. Jesus said, "Love your _____."

    enemies   vacation   homework

5. What is one thing you will tell Jesus today?

FAITH ALIVE ▪ AT HOME AND IN THE PARISH

In this lesson your child met Jesus as our friend and healer. Jesus reached out to everyone He met and affirmed the goodness in each one. That is being a healer! He healed physical ailments but even more importantly, He healed spiritual sicknesses with the healing touch of forgiveness. We can experience the healing of Jesus in the sacraments of Reconciliation, Eucharist, and Anointing of the Sick, as well as in the Christian community, in works of charity and justice, and in prayer.

The Gift of Friendship

Talk with your child about Jesus as our best friend. Invite him or her to sing the song about Jesus as our best friend (page 104). Share ways your family can show friendship and healing to others in your neighborhood and parish.

11 Jesus Is Our Teacher

Jesus, teach us to love.

Our Life

Read to me
In the school bus yesterday Lia taught me a hand game. Lia said, "Dad taught me last night. He said my grandmother taught it to him when he was our age."

Now I can't wait to show my cousin the next time I see him.

Talk about some good things your family has taught you.

What can you teach a friend?

Sharing Life

Do you like to learn new things from others? Why?

Do you like to share what you learn? Why?

Can you think of something Jesus has taught you?

106

Learn this hand poem about Jesus.
Practice it with a partner.
Then teach it to someone at home.

Jesus teaches me to love
(1)   (2)   (3)

God and everyone.
(4)   (5)

If we love as Jesus does,
(5)   (3)   (1)

Love will make us one.
(3)   (5) (6)

In this lesson we will discover what
Jesus teaches us about love.

We Will Learn

- God is our loving Father.

- Jesus teaches us the Law of Love.

- God's love will last forever.

Begin by praying the prayer-poem you learned yesterday.

Who loves and cares for you? How?

God Is Like a Loving Parent

One day Jesus wanted to teach the people about God's love for them. He told them to think about their parents.

Parents love their children. They care for them always. Jesus taught people that God is like a loving father. God loves us and cares for us, no matter what we do.

One day Jesus' friends said, "Teach us to pray." Jesus said, "When you pray, call God 'Father.'"

From Luke 11:1–2

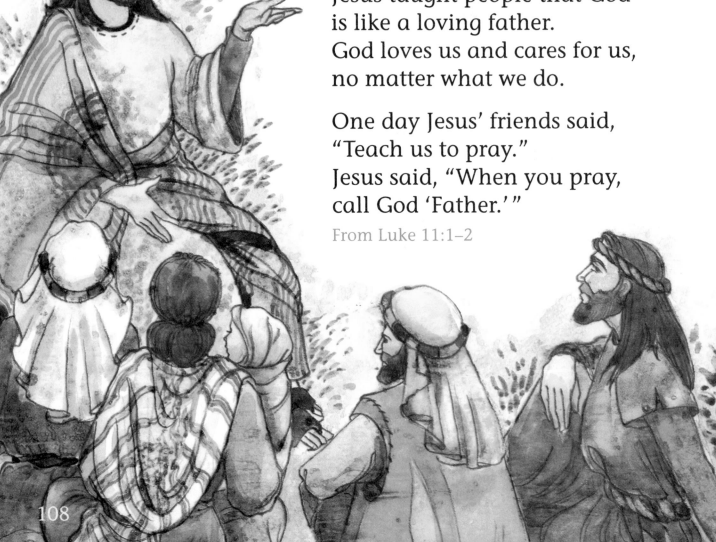

Here is the prayer Jesus taught them.

Our Father, who art in heaven,
hallowed be thy name;
thy kingdom come;
thy will be done on earth
as it is in heaven.
Give us this day our daily bread;
and forgive us our trespasses
as we forgive those
who trespass against us;
and lead us not into temptation,
but deliver us from evil. Amen.

Decorate the Our Father when
you have learned it by heart.

How did Jesus teach
us to pray?

Pray the Our Father
now together.

109

OUR CATHOLIC FAITH

- Begin by praying the Our Father together.

- What does it mean for you to really love someone?

The Law of Love

Jesus wants us to love God, and to love others as we love ourselves.

Read to me from the Bible

One day, a man came to Jesus. He asked Jesus how God wants us to live. Jesus said, "Love God above all things. Love other people as you love yourself."

From Mark 12:30–31

This is how God wants us to live. We call it the Law of Love. We are to show our love for God by loving others as we love ourselves.

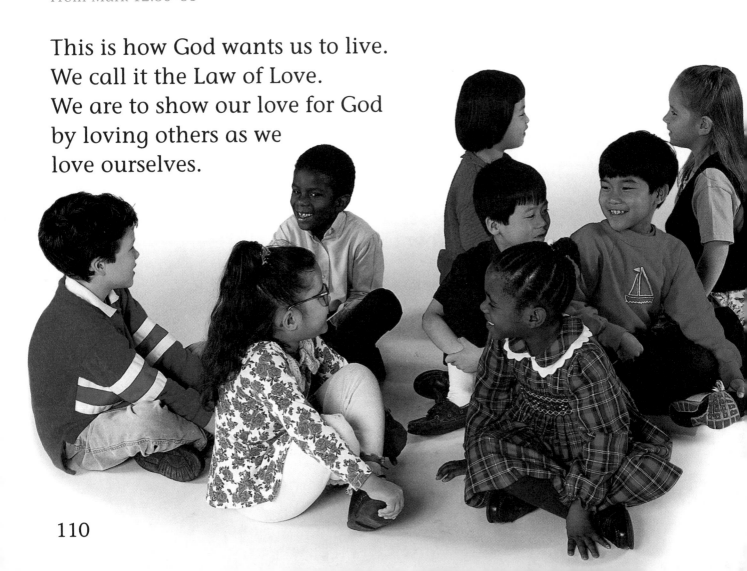

Of all the good things that we can do, Jesus said love is the best thing of all.

What a happy world this would be if everyone loved God, loved all people, and loved themselves!

Gather together with your friends. Say to the person next to you, "You are God's child. I love you."

Draw yourself and a friend on this page.

The **Law of Love** teaches us to love God, and others as we love ourselves.

■ What do you think it means to love yourself?

■ Will you ask God to help you love yourself? What will you say?

OUR CATHOLIC FAITH

Dear God, help us to live the Law of Love.

Why do you think God will love you forever?

God's Love Lasts Forever

God knows you by name and loves you. God will never stop loving you. His love lasts forever.

Read to me from the Bible

Once Jesus said, "Look how God loves the birds. He feeds and cares for them. Look how God loves the flowers. He made them so beautiful."

Then Jesus said, "God loves you much more than the birds and the flowers."

From Matthew 6:26–32

Praying Hands

Some people pray with their hands folded. Others have their hands outstretched. Still others hold hands. Can you tell other ways we can use our bodies to pray to God?

Tell about the different ways and times you like to pray. Draw a picture that shows one of the ways and times you like to pray.

It could be your morning and evening prayers, your mealtime prayers, prayers at Mass, or when you are alone.

Learn by heart **Faith Summary**

- God is like a loving parent.

- Jesus taught us the Law of Love.

Coming To Faith

Here are some ways Jesus taught us to love.

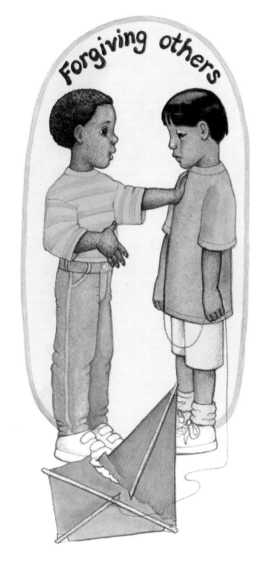

Forgiving others

Being kind to the poor

Join your hands in a circle.
Take turns going into the middle of the circle.
Act out how we can show love.
See if your friends can name each loving way.

Practicing Faith

Stay in your friendship circle.
Pray the Our Father together.

Pray this prayer at Mass with the people in your parish.
Practice saying the Our Father until you know it by heart.

Praying to God

Talk with the children about ways they might share the "Faith Alive" section with their families. Pray the Our Father together as a closing faith response.

REVIEW ■ TEST

Circle the correct answer.

1. We are to love God and others as we love ourselves. This is the Law of _____ .

Life   Love   Bible

2. The prayer Jesus taught is the _____ .

Alleluia   Hail Mary   Our Father

3. God's love for us will _____ .

end   last forever   last a day

4. Tell one way that Jesus taught us to love.

FAITH ALIVE AT HOME AND IN THE PARISH

In this lesson your child learned the great Law of Love, which teaches that we must love God above all things and must love others as we love ourselves. It is often called the great commandment. Your child has also learned the Our Father—the prayer that Jesus Himself taught. The *Catechism of the Catholic Church* reminds us that the Our Father is a summary of the whole gospel and the model for Christian prayer.

The Law of Love

Talk with your child about the Law of Love and what it means to you. Then share together ways you will show love this week for

■ God
■ others
■ yourself

The Our Father

Invite your child to pray the Our Father with you. Help him or her with the difficult words. This week during Mass help your child to join your parish community in praying it together before Holy Communion.

12 Jesus Gives Us Himself

Thank You, Jesus, for giving us Yourself.

OUR LIFE

Some grandmas and grandpas live far away.
Here are ways to tell them we love them.

Phone a kiss.

Mail a hug.

Write a card.

Say a prayer.

Circle one you can do.
What else can you do?

Will it make your Grandma or Grandpa happy?

SHARING LIFE

How do you remember your friends when they are away?

Does Jesus want you to remember Him? Tell why.

What do you like to remember best about Jesus? Why?

Work together to make a "We Remember Jesus" book. Here are some ideas for the book.

- Draw a picture of your favorite story about Jesus.

- Write a prayer to Jesus.

- Draw a picture of yourself with Jesus.

Put the pages of the book together. Make a cover for the book. Keep it where everyone can look at it and remember Jesus.

In this lesson we will discover what Jesus did to help us remember He is with us always.

We Will Learn

- Jesus gave us Himself at the Last Supper.

- Jesus died and rose from the dead.

- Jesus promised to give us a Helper, the Holy Spirit.

117

OUR CATHOLIC FAITH

■ Jesus, thank You for being with us always.

■ What is the best way to remember Jesus?

The Last Supper

Jesus wanted us to remember Him. Jesus wanted to be with us always. This is what He did.

Read to me from the Bible

The night before Jesus died, He had a special meal with His friends. We call this meal the Last Supper.

During the meal, Jesus took bread. He gave thanks to God. He broke the bread. He gave it to His friends and said, "This is My Body."

Jesus took a cup of wine. He gave thanks again. He gave the cup to His friends and said, "This is the cup of My Blood."

The bread and wine became the Body and Blood of Jesus.

Then Jesus said, "Do this in memory of Me."
From Luke 22:14–20

We call this day Holy Thursday.

Jesus gives us the gift of Himself at Mass. He gives us His Body and Blood. We call the Body and Blood of Christ Holy Communion.

Holy Communion is the Body and Blood of Christ.

When you are ready, you will receive Jesus in Holy Communion.

Imagine you are at the Last Supper. Draw yourself at the table.

- Tell about the special gift that Jesus gave us.
- Thank You, Jesus, for giving us the gift of Yourself.

119

Jesus, You are always with Your friends.

Tell what happened at the Last Supper.

Jesus Dies and Rises

This is what happened after the Last Supper.

Read to me from the Bible

After the Last Supper, Jesus and His friends went into a garden. Jesus prayed to God His Father. Soldiers came and took Him away. Some people said Jesus had taught, "I am God's Son!" They did not believe Jesus' words. They said Jesus had to die for saying He was God's Son.

From Matthew 26:36–66

Jesus was nailed to a cross and died for us. Jesus' mother and some friends were by the cross. They stayed with Him until He died.

From John 19:18–30

We call this day Good Friday. It is the day Jesus gave His life for us. Jesus is our Savior.

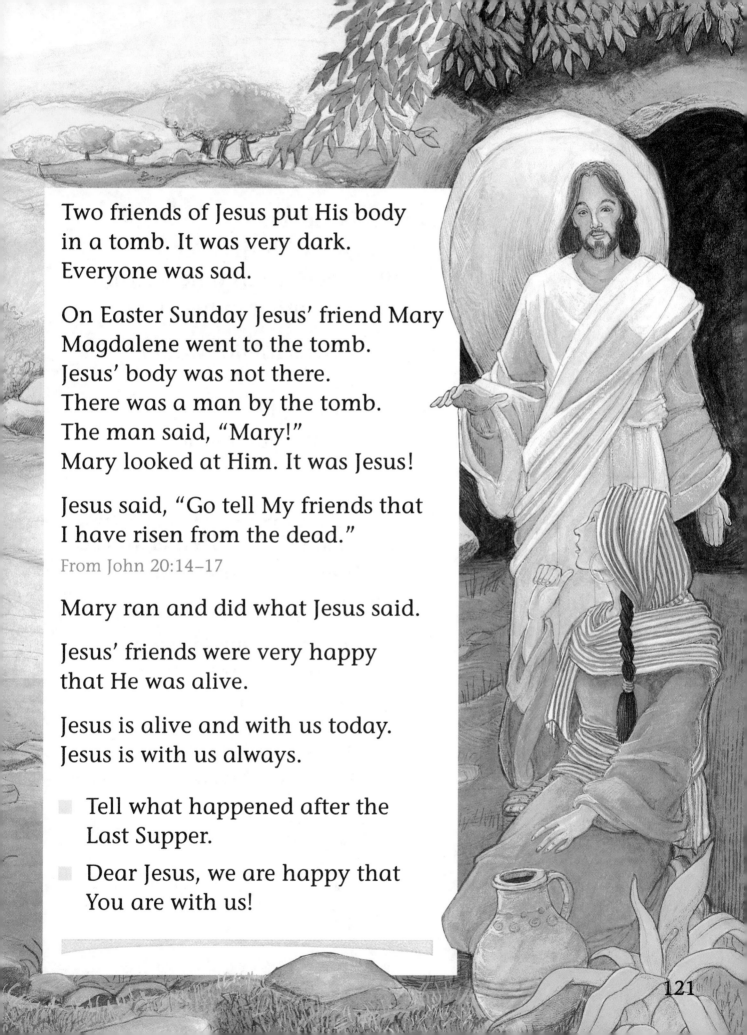

Two friends of Jesus put His body in a tomb. It was very dark. Everyone was sad.

On Easter Sunday Jesus' friend Mary Magdalene went to the tomb. Jesus' body was not there. There was a man by the tomb. The man said, "Mary!" Mary looked at Him. It was Jesus!

Jesus said, "Go tell My friends that I have risen from the dead."

From John 20:14–17

Mary ran and did what Jesus said.

Jesus' friends were very happy that He was alive.

Jesus is alive and with us today. Jesus is with us always.

- Tell what happened after the Last Supper.

- Dear Jesus, we are happy that You are with us!

121

Our Catholic Faith

- Jesus is risen, alleluia!
- Tell the story of Easter Sunday.

The Holy Spirit

Jesus stayed with His friends for a while. Then it was time for Him to go to His Father in heaven.

Jesus knew His friends would need help.
He said, "Do not be afraid. I will not leave you alone."

From John 14:16

Jesus promised to send His friends a special Helper. The Helper would remind them of all Jesus had told them.

The Helper that Jesus sent was the Holy Spirit, the third Person of the Blessed Trinity.

God the Holy Spirit helps us today to live as friends of Jesus.

A Saint Named John

One of Jesus' followers was John. John always wanted to be close to Jesus.

When Jesus was dying on the cross some of His followers were afraid and ran away. But John did not leave. He stayed by the cross with Mary, the mother of Jesus, and some of the women disciples.

After the women disciples, John was one of the first to know that Jesus was risen from the dead.

This wonderful friend of Jesus is Saint John.

Ask Saint John to help us to stay close to Jesus, too.

Learn by heart Faith Summary

- Jesus gives us the gift of Himself in Holy Communion.

- Jesus died and rose from the dead.

123

Coming To Faith

Imagine you and your friends are
at the Last Supper.
Tell what you hear Jesus say.

Then be very quiet.
Put your right hand over your heart.
Tell Jesus how you feel.

Practicing Faith

Listen at Mass for the story of
what Jesus did at the Last Supper.

Think of something to do this week
to thank Jesus for the gift of Himself.

Talk to the children about ways they
and their families might share the
"Faith Alive" section. Encourage the
children to do the Gifts for Mass
activity with a family member.

REVIEW ▪ TEST

Fill in the circle beside the correct answer.

1. God raised Jesus from the dead on _____.

○ Easter   ○ Holy Thursday   ○ Good Friday

2. Jesus gave His Body and Blood at _____.

○ the tomb   ○ the Last Supper   ○ Christmas

3. We receive Jesus' Body and Blood _____.

○ in the Bible   ○ in Holy Communion   ○ on the cross

4. Tell in your own words what happened at the Last Supper.

FAITH ALIVE AT HOME AND IN THE PARISH

In this lesson your child learned about what happened on Holy Thursday (the Last Supper), Good Friday (the crucifixion), and Easter Sunday (the resurrection). The time from Holy Thursday evening to Easter Sunday evening is called the Easter Triduum. The Triduum is the most important time in the Church's liturgical year. Because of Jesus' death and resurrection, we share His new life. Every one of us is called to pass from death to eternal life.

The Last Supper

Help your child make a drawing showing what Jesus did at the Last Supper. Let him or her tell you what is in the picture. At Mass this week remind your child to listen carefully for the story of what Jesus did at the Last Supper. You might alert your child to listen well as the Eucharistic Prayer begins.

Gifts for Mass

Invite each family member to think of and to do one act of love to offer to Jesus at Mass this week.

13   Advent

Come,
Lord Jesus!

OUR LIFE

Read to me

Nana is coming
To visit tonight,
When the stars are out
And the moon is bright.

It's Nana's birthday
So we cleaned all day,
Getting ready for her
In a special way.

I'm so excited!
I can hardly wait!
When Nana's here,
We'll celebrate.

Do you ever help get ready
for a special celebration?
What do you do?

SHARING LIFE

What do you like best about celebrations?

How do you feel when you are waiting
to celebrate? Tell about it.

126

Here is a story about waiting.
Act it out with your friends.

Read to me

Tim and Emily pressed their faces against the window pane. Their dad had been away for a long time. Now he was coming home. He should be coming up the walk right now! The children ran and looked at the clock. They pestered their mother, "Where's Dad? Why isn't he here?"

Their mother said, "Be patient. Everything is ready. Dad will be here soon."

Emily and Tim ran back to the window. Who was that? Someone big and smiling was coming up the walk....

What do you think Emily and Tim did?

Tell about a time when you got ready to welcome someone.

In this lesson we will get ready to celebrate the coming of Jesus.

We Will Learn

- Advent is a time of waiting and preparing for Jesus.

- We prepare for Jesus in special ways.

Do you remember the Bible story of the first man and woman? They turned away from God. But God did not stop loving them. God promised to send someone to show people how to live as His friends.

The people waited many, many years. God kept His promise by sending His own Son, Jesus.

Each year we remember and celebrate Jesus' birth on Christmas. We continue to wait until Jesus will come again. Advent is the name we give to our waiting time before Christmas.

We do things to get ready for
the coming of Jesus. We pray to Jesus.
We light candles to remind us that
Jesus is our light. Jesus will come into our
hearts in a special way at Christmas.

Read the words of this Advent
message from the Bible.

Come, Jesus, come!
May the Lord Jesus
be with everyone.

Revelation 22:20–21

Coming To Faith

Sing this song during the four weeks of Advent. It will help you pray to Jesus as you get ready for Christmas.
(To the tune of "Twinkle, Twinkle")

♫Jesus, Jesus, be our light.
Come to make the darkness bright.
Jesus, come and guide our way,
Help us care and share each day.
Jesus, Jesus, be our light.
Come to make the darkness bright.♫

Practicing Faith

How will you help and share in Advent? The pictures may help you decide.

Make an Advent calendar.
Color a star each day you do something to light the way for Jesus.

130

Talk to the children about ways they and their families might use the "Faith Alive" section. Then sing the Advent song as a closing faith response.

REVIEW ■ TEST

Circle **Yes** or **No**.
If you are not sure, circle **?**.

1. Advent is the same as Christmas.   **Yes**   **No**   **?**

2. Candles remind us that Jesus
is our light.   **Yes**   **No**   **?**

3. God kept His promise by
sending Jesus.   **Yes**   **No**   **?**

4. In Advent we prepare for Easter.   **Yes**   **No**   **?**

5. Tell one thing you will do to prepare
to celebrate Jesus' birth.

FAITH ALIVE AT HOME AND IN THE PARISH

In this lesson your child was introduced to the liturgical season of Advent as a time of waiting and preparing for Jesus. For Catholics Advent has a dual purpose. It is a time to prepare for Christmas, when we celebrate the first coming of God's Son. It is also a time to turn our minds to Christ's second coming at the end of time. It is, therefore, a season of joy and expectation.

Learn by heart **Faith Summary**

• Advent is a time of waiting to celebrate Jesus' birth at Christmas.

• We prepare for Christmas by praying and helping others.

131

14 | Christmas

Jesus,
we welcome You
into our hearts.

OUR LIFE

Sing "Silent Night" very softly.
We wish to welcome Jesus into our hearts.

♫ Silent night, holy night,
　All is calm, all is bright;
　Round yon Virgin Mother and Child!
　Holy Infant so tender and mild,
　Sleep in heavenly peace,
　Sleep in heavenly peace. ♫

Tell about your feelings as you sing
this song.
What do the words of the song say
about the night Jesus was born?

SHARING LIFE

Imagine you are there in Bethlehem
on the first Christmas.
Tell what you see and hear.

Now pretend you are one of the people in the picture. Think of something you can bring as a gift for Jesus. Your gift can be something you will do to help at home, in your neighborhood, at school, or in your parish.

Write or draw on a sheet of paper the one thing you will do. Share it with a friend.

Put your gift under your tree for Jesus.

In this lesson we will act out the story of Jesus' birth.

We Will Learn

- Jesus brings us light and love.

- Jesus wants us to share love with others.

133

A Christmas Play

Narrator: In those days, a letter went out from the king that all the people should be counted. Mary and Joseph went to Bethlehem to do this. Mary was expecting a baby.

Joseph: Mary, we are almost there. You must be tired. Let's stop at the inn. (knocks at the door)

Innkeeper: What do you want?

Joseph: We need a place to rest.

Innkeeper: There is no room for you here. You can stay in the stable in the back.

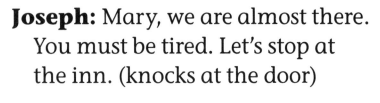

Narrator: So Joseph and Mary went to the stable. During the night, Jesus was born. Nearby shepherds were caring for their sheep. Suddenly a bright light filled the sky. Angels appeared to them.

Angels: Do not be afraid. We have good news. The Savior is born. You will find a baby in a stable in Bethlehem.

Narrator: The shepherds went to Bethlehem. They found Mary, Joseph, and the baby Jesus in the stable.

From Luke 2:1–16

Coming To Faith

Jesus came to bring us light and love. We want to share His light and love with others. Let us make a Christmas candle.

Gather around the Christmas crib, with your candle, as we pray.

✝**Leader:** Welcome, Jesus, into our hearts today and always.
All: Welcome, Jesus, into our hearts.

Leader: Help us share the light of Your love with others.
All: Welcome, Jesus, into our world.

All: Sing "Silent Night" prayerfully.

PRACTICING FAITH

Jesus is with us today. How will you share
Jesus' light and love with others on
Christmas and every day?
Draw one of
the ways here.

Take a few minutes to
talk with the children
about ways they and
their families might use
the "Faith Alive" sec-
tion. Encourage them
to say their Christmas
prayer during the
Christmas season.

REVIEW ■ TEST

Show the order in which the story happened.
Put a number in the box beside each sentence.

One box is done for you.

☐ The shepherds found Mary, Joseph, and the baby Jesus in the stable.

1 Mary and Joseph went to Bethlehem to be counted.

☐ Angels told good news to the shepherds.

☐ During the night Jesus was born.

☐ There was no room at the inn so Mary and Joseph went to a stable.

Come, Holy Spirit! Help us to live as friends of Jesus.

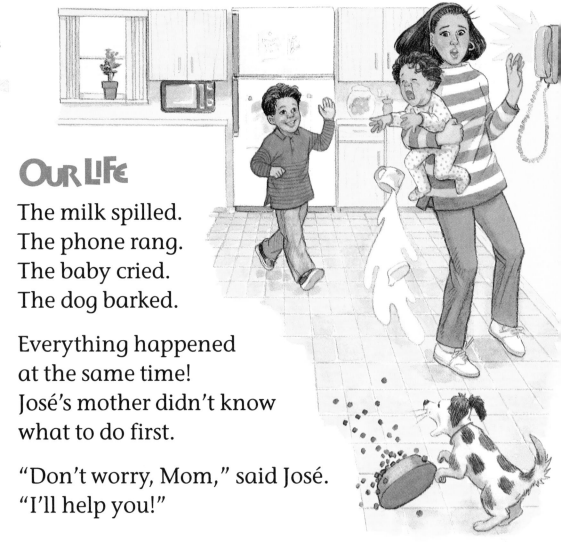

Our Life

The milk spilled.
The phone rang.
The baby cried.
The dog barked.

Everything happened
at the same time!
José's mother didn't know
what to do first.

"Don't worry, Mom," said José.
"I'll help you!"

Finish the story. Name some things that
José could do to help.

Tell about times when you help someone.

Sharing Life

Tell about a time when you needed
someone to help you.
Do you ever ask God for help?

Choose a friendship partner.
Tell each other about times
when you asked for God's help.

Pray to God for each other.
Take turns putting your hands
on each other's head.

Then pray,
† God, this is my friend

_____.

(your partner's name)

Help my friend to know
Your love always.

In this lesson we will discover
that Jesus sent the Holy Spirit
to be our Helper.

We Will Learn
- The Holy Spirit came to the friends of Jesus.
- The Holy Spirit helped the friends of Jesus.
- The Holy Spirit helped the Church to begin.

139

■ Close your eyes. Be very still. Ask God to help you in all you do and say.

■ Why do we need God's help?

The Holy Spirit Comes

Jesus knew that after He left His friends they would need a Helper. Jesus promised them, "I will send you a Helper. The Holy Spirit will help you remember all that I have said."

From John 14:26

Here is the Bible story of how Jesus kept His promise.

Read to me from the Bible

The friends of Jesus were waiting for the Helper Jesus had promised. Mary, the mother of Jesus, was with them.

The **Holy Spirit** is God, the third Person of the Blessed Trinity.

Suddenly they heard a loud noise like a wind blowing. They saw what looked like flames of fire touching each one.

The Helper, the Holy Spirit, had come! The friends of Jesus were filled with God the Holy Spirit.

Then the friends of Jesus ran outside into the street. They told all the people the good news of Jesus.
From Acts 2:2–6

God the Holy Spirit helped the friends of Jesus to remember everything Jesus had said and done.

The Holy Spirit is with us today. The Holy Spirit helps us to live as Jesus taught us.

Act out what happened when the Holy Spirit came.

- How does God the Holy Spirit help you?

- What will you ask the Holy Spirit to help you do today?

OUR CATHOLIC FAITH

■ Holy Spirit, teach us. Help us to do what is right.

■ When do you need help to live as a friend of Jesus?

The Holy Spirit the Helper

After Jesus went away,
His friends were afraid.
They were afraid that
they might be killed, too.
The Holy Spirit helped them
not to be afraid.

God the Holy Spirit also
helped the friends of Jesus
in many other ways.
The Holy Spirit helped them
to pray every day.

The Holy Spirit was with them
when they shared the Body
and Blood of Christ in Holy
Communion.

The Holy Spirit helped them to remember to love others as Jesus taught. The Holy Spirit helped them to be peacemakers.

The friends of Jesus shared what they had. No one was hungry. Each had a place to stay.

Everyone said, "See how these Christians love one another." Christians are followers of Jesus.

The Holy Spirit helps us, too. The Holy Spirit helps us to live as friends of Jesus.

Write and learn
"See how these Christians

_____

- -

_____

one another."

What did the Holy Spirit do for the friends of Jesus?

How will you ask the Holy Spirit to help you?

OUR CATHOLIC FAITH

■ Holy Spirit, help us to live as followers of Jesus.

■ Why do you think it is important to belong to the Church?

The Church Begins

The Holy Spirit helped the first Christians to tell everyone the good news of Jesus.

More and more people believed in Jesus Christ. They came together as Jesus' Church.

The Church is Jesus and His baptized friends joined together by the Holy Spirit.

The Holy Spirit helped the Church to begin. The Holy Spirit still helps the Church today to do the work of Jesus.

You are a follower of Jesus Christ. You are a member of His Church. The Holy Spirit helps you to live as a Christian, too.

Sing Your Joy!

Catholics like to come together to celebrate as Jesus' friends. We do this especially at Mass each weekend with our parish family.

Sometimes we sing songs together to tell God what is in our hearts.
Singing songs to God is a beautiful way to pray. Do you have a favorite song to sing to God? Tell about it.

Now sing one of your favorite songs together. Tell God how happy you are to be Jesus' friends.

Learn by heart **Faith Summary**

- The Holy Spirit came to the friends of Jesus.

- The Holy Spirit helped the Church to begin and helps us today.

Coming To Faith

Act out the story about how Jesus kept His promise to send the Holy Spirit.

What help did the Holy Spirit give the first Christians?

How can the Holy Spirit help you today?

Practicing Faith

Close your eyes. Imagine you are the streamers in the picture. Stand still waiting for the wind. Then flutter and fly gently in the wind.

Sway back and forth or twirl around. Pray to the Holy Spirit as you move.

✝ Holy Spirit, help me today in all I think and do and say!

Will you say this prayer each day this week?

146

Talk with the children about ways they and their families might use the "Faith Alive" section. Encourage them to share their Holy Spirit prayer with someone at home.

REVIEW ■ TEST

Fill in the circle beside the correct answer.

1. Jesus sent the _____ to the church.
   ○ Christians   ○ Blessed Trinity   ○ Holy Spirit

2. The Holy Spirit is God, the third Person of _____.
   ○ Christians   ○ the Church   ○ the Blessed Trinity

3. The Holy Spirit helps the Church to do
   the work of _____.
   ○ Jesus Christ   ○ the Helper   ○ Mary

4. Tell the story of the coming of the Holy Spirit.

FAITH ALIVE AT HOME AND IN THE PARISH

This week your child learned about God the Holy Spirit, the third Person of the Blessed Trinity. The Holy Spirit is the Helper Jesus promised to send His disciples. After the death of Jesus, the disciples were filled with doubt, fear, and regret. But when the Holy Spirit came upon them on Pentecost, they were filled with confidence and courage to proclaim openly and fearlessly their faith in Jesus Christ. The Holy Spirit helps us every day to live and witness to our faith in Jesus Christ.

A Picture Story

Talk with your child about times when he or she might need the help of the Holy Spirit. Invite your child to draw one of these times. Have your child tell about the drawing. Encourage your child to ask the Holy Spirit for help in times like these.

† A Prayer to the Holy Spirit

Come, Holy Spirit, fill the hearts of Your faithful and enkindle in them the fire of Your love.

Jesus, how good it is to belong to Your Church!

OUR LIFE

Look at the picture of all the animals working together.

What do you think they are trying to do?

How is each animal helping?

Do you like to work with others?

What team or group do you belong to?

What do you do?

SHARING LIFE

Why do people sometimes need to work together?

Why should friends of Jesus work together?

Friends of Jesus

Tell what the children in this picture are doing to show they are friends of Jesus.

Imagine that you go to this school. Decide what your group can do as friends of Jesus. Write it on the blank sign.

In this lesson we will discover what it means to be friends of Jesus in the Church.

We Will Learn

- The Holy Spirit helped Paul to follow Jesus.

- We are members of the Church.

- The Church is for everyone.

149

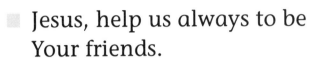
- Jesus, help us always to be Your friends.

- Tell how the friends of Jesus should work together.

Paul Joins the Church

The friends of Jesus told many people about Him. The Holy Spirit helped these people to believe in Jesus and become His friends, too.

These new friends of Jesus wanted to join the group of Jesus' followers. They were baptized and became Christians. They became members of Jesus' Church.

One of Jesus' special friends was a man named Paul. Paul was not always Jesus' friend.

At first Paul was very mean to people who were followers of Jesus. But then the Holy Spirit helped Paul to know that Jesus was really the Son of God.

From that time on, Paul told people
everywhere about Jesus.
Paul became a great leader
in the Church.
We call him Saint Paul.

Paul taught people that Jesus'
Church was for everyone.
Anyone who believed in Jesus and
wanted to be His follower could
be baptized and become a Christian.
Baptized Christians are members
of Jesus' Church.

■ How did people join Jesus'
Church?

■ Tell how you can be like
Saint Paul.

151

OUR CATHOLIC FAITH

■ Saint Paul, help us to be strong members of the Church.

■ Tell something that you know Jesus wants you to do.

We Belong to Jesus' Church

Jesus wants us to love God and to live as His followers. Jesus said, "Love one another just as I have loved you."

From John 15:12

When Jesus saw that people were hungry, He fed them. If people were sad, He became their friend.

When Jesus saw sick people, He helped them. He cared about poor people. Jesus was fair to everyone. He helped people to live in peace.

We are followers of Jesus Christ.
We are Christians.
We belong to the Church.

We try to live as Jesus did. We try to show our love for one another. This is what it means to be followers of Jesus.

We follow Jesus as members of the Catholic Church. We can pray and be kind to others. We can play fair and be peacemakers.

Trace and wear a button that says, "I belong to the Church."

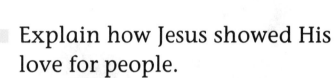

Explain how Jesus showed His love for people.

How can you show that you are a follower of Jesus today?

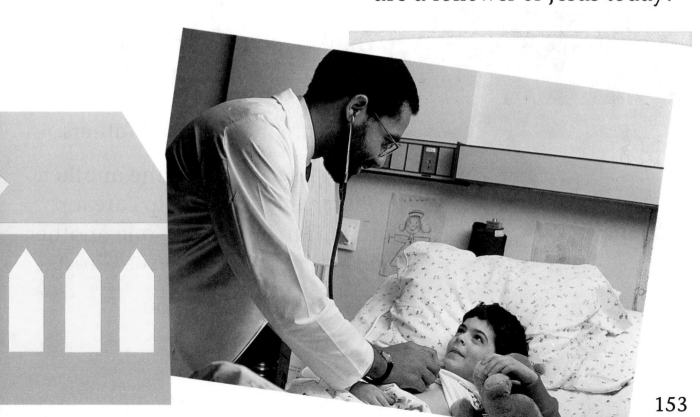

OUR CATHOLIC FAITH

■ Stand in a prayer circle wearing your buttons. Pray together: Jesus, help us to love one another.

■ Who can be a follower of Jesus?

The Church Is for Everyone

Jesus invites everyone to belong to His Church. Everyone in the Church is important.

People serve the Church in different ways. Our Holy Father, the pope, is the leader of the whole Catholic Church. Bishops, priests, and deacons serve the Church. Many other people serve the Church, too.

Think of all the people who help in your parish. Some take care of the sick. Some are teachers. Some are mothers and fathers.

All of us try to help one another. All of us together help care for the Church. We help one another live as followers of Jesus Christ.

The Church needs you.

Church

Tell what comes to your mind when you hear the word Church. Maybe you thought of a building with a cross. Maybe you thought of going to Mass. Did you ever think of people?

The Church is not just a building or a celebration. It is all the baptized people who believe in God and in Jesus Christ, the Son of God.

This means we are the Church. The Church is the people of God. All over the world the people of God believe and worship and care for others.

Tell how you are part of the Church.

Learn by heart **Faith Summary**

● Jesus invites everyone to belong to His Church.

● We are part of the Church and try to treat others as Jesus did.

COMING TO FAITH

Who is the leader
of the whole Church?

Can you name someone
else who helps the Church?
What does this person do?

Tell how you feel about
belonging to the Church.

PRACTICING FAITH

Tell what you will do
if each of these happens:

- A classmate forgets lunch.

- A new classmate
  is lonely and afraid.

- Someone is calling
  someone else bad names.

- Your younger brother
  or sister wants you to play.

Tell what you will do today
to show that you follow Jesus.

Talk to the children about ways they
and their families might use the
"Faith Alive" section. Encourage them
to visit their parish church with a
family member.

REVIEW ■ TEST

Fill in the circle beside the correct answer.

1. Jesus invites everyone in the world to belong to _____ .

○ my parish   ○ the pope   ○ the Church

2. The leader of the whole Catholic Church is _____ .

○ our pastor   ○ the pope   ○ the Holy Spirit

3. All the followers of Jesus are called _____ .

○ Americans   ○ Fathers   ○ Christians

4. How did Jesus say we should "love one another"?

FAITH ALIVE AT HOME AND IN THE PARISH

In this lesson your child learned how we are to live as Jesus' followers and members of His Church. He or she learned that Jesus said, "Love one another just as I have loved you" (John 15:12). We call this the new commandment. One way to help young children grow as followers of Jesus Christ is to provide them with consistent examples of Christian values such as patience, truthfulness, honesty, compassion, justice, and love. We can also be models for them by saying "I'm sorry" and asking for forgiveness when we are wrong or hurt someone.

Parish Helpers

Each person in your parish has different talents. Discuss with your child the different talents that people share to make the parish a special place. Help your child identify that he or she can do many things to help the parish and school. Take time to name a few.

A Visit to Our Church

Take your child to visit your parish church during the week. Bless yourselves with holy water at the door, then go to the place where the Blessed Sacrament is reserved. Genuflect and pray a short prayer together to Jesus, who is present in the Blessed Sacrament. Then walk around the church noticing the statues, the stations of the cross, and the stained-glass windows. Talk quietly about what you see.

17 The Church Celebrates Baptism

Our Life

Read to me

Janie watched the priest place Anthony in the water. She listened to all the words. When the Baptism was over, the priest said, "Anthony is now a child of God. Let us welcome him into the Church." Everyone clapped. Janie's mother turned to her and said, "Janie, you are a child of God too."

Janie was excited.
"I'm a child of God, too!" she said.

Can you tell how you feel about being a child of God?

Sharing Life

Tell why you think your family wanted you to become a child of God.

Make a reminder of your Baptism.
Trace and color this baptismal font.
On the back, print

" _____

(your name)
is a child of God."

Bring your reminder home.
Ask your family to tell you about
the day of your Baptism.

In this lesson we will discover what
it means to be children of God.

We Will Learn

- Baptism makes us children of God.

- We celebrate Baptism.

- We live as followers of Jesus.

Stand and say in a loud voice:
"We are God's children!"
Clap to show how glad you are.

Explain what you think
happened at your Baptism.

Baptism Makes Us God's Children

Jesus wants everyone to be a
child of God. He wants everyone
to have God's own life and love.

When we are baptized, we
become God's own children.
We receive God's own life
and love. We call this grace.
We become part of the Church.
You are baptized. You share
in God's life and love.
You are God's child.
You belong to the Church.

160

Baptism gives us God's own life and love.

The Holy Spirit is with you.
The Holy Spirit helps you to live as Jesus taught us.

From John 14:16–17

We try to live the way Jesus taught.

Draw yourself in this picture.

- Are you happy that you are baptized? Why?

- Make up a prayer asking the Holy Spirit to help you today.

161

OUR CATHOLIC FAITH

■ Dear God, thank You for Your life and love in us.

■ Why do families celebrate when they have a child baptized?

We Celebrate Baptism

Catholic parents want their babies to become children of God through Baptism. They bring their babies to their parish church.

The priest and all the people welcome them. Everyone prays for the baby and the family.

The priest baptizes the baby with water. He says,

✝ "I baptize you in the name of the Father, and of the Son, and of the Holy Spirit."

The baby now has God's life of grace. The baby is a child of God and a member of Jesus' Church.

Act out a Baptism. Paste a picture here.

■ How does it make you feel to be a child of God?

■ What will you do today to show you are a child of God?

OUR CATHOLIC FAITH

- To thank God for our Baptism, let us make the sign of the cross together.

- Tell some things you do because you are baptized.

We Live As Jesus Did

After the first Christians were baptized, they wanted everyone to know the good news of Jesus.

The Holy Spirit helped them to tell others about Jesus. The Holy Spirit helped them to live as Jesus taught.

We are baptized, too. We can tell everyone about Jesus.
The Holy Spirit helps us to live as friends of Jesus.

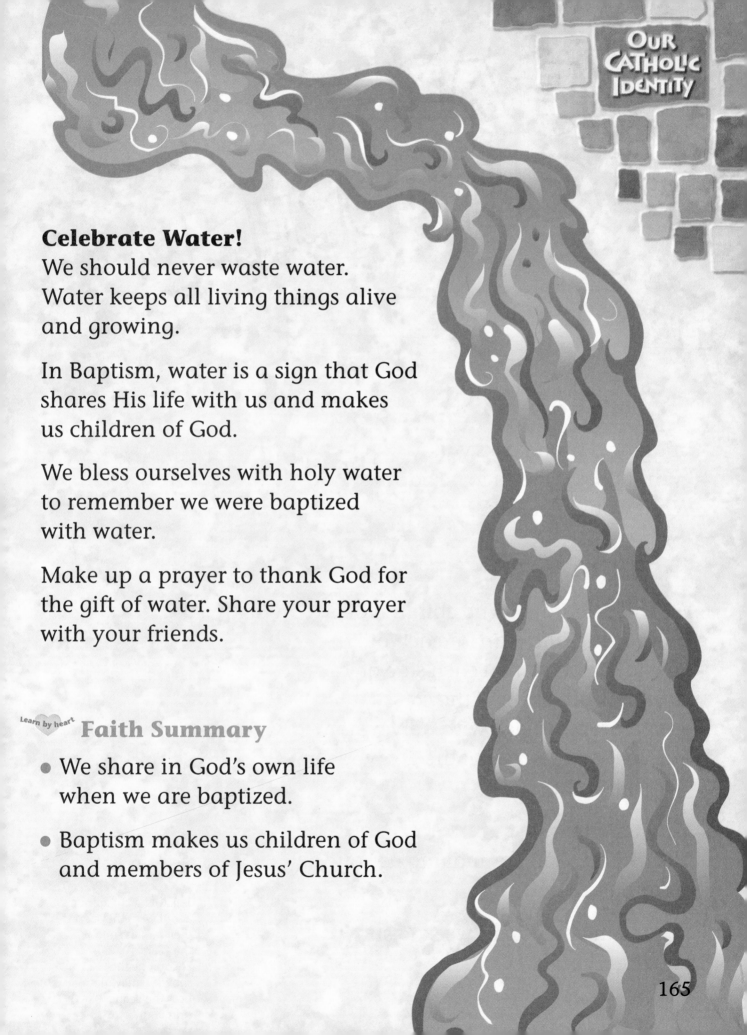

Celebrate Water!

We should never waste water. Water keeps all living things alive and growing.

In Baptism, water is a sign that God shares His life with us and makes us children of God.

We bless ourselves with holy water to remember we were baptized with water.

Make up a prayer to thank God for the gift of water. Share your prayer with your friends.

Learn by heart ## Faith Summary

- We share in God's own life when we are baptized.

- Baptism makes us children of God and members of Jesus' Church.

165

WE ARE GOD'S CHILDREN

COMING TO FAITH

Imagine a friend asks you,
"What does it mean to be baptized?"
What would you say?

PRACTICING FAITH

We will celebrate being children of God.
Let us stand and clap for each other.
Bow to the person on each side of you.
Now make the sign of the cross
as you are sprinkled with holy water.
This will remind you of the day you
were baptized.

Pray together,
✝ Thank You, God, for making us Your
children in Baptism.

What can you do this week to show
you are a child of God?

166

Talk to the children
about ways they and
their families might use
the "Faith Alive" section.
Encourage them to
show a family member
how they can make the
sign of the cross.

REVIEW ■ TEST

Fill in the circle beside the correct answer.

1. _____ gives us God's own life and love.

⃝ Prayer   ⃝ Baptism   ⃝ Water

2. In Baptism we receive God's special life
of _____ .

⃝ grace   ⃝ water   ⃝ parish

3. The priest pours _____ over the baby's head.

⃝ Jesus   ⃝ light   ⃝ water

4. Tell one thing you will do to show you are
God's child.

FAITH ALIVE ■ AT HOME AND IN THE PARISH

In this lesson your child learned that Baptism gives us a share of God's own life and love. We call this grace. Through Baptism we are freed from the slavery of sin and welcomed as members of the Church, the body of Christ. Explain to your child that every baptized person has the responsibility to live as a follower of Jesus. This means that we live our faith in Jesus every day. It also means caring for those in need and those who are treated unjustly. Your example in living your own Baptism will help your child grow in living the faith.

Sign of the Cross

You might want to recall and share your memories about your child's baptismal day. Make the sign of the cross as you bless yourself and your child with holy water. Explain to your child that this reminds us of the water used on our Baptism day.

18 The Church Celebrates
(The Mass Begins)

Thank You,
Jesus,
for the Mass.

Our Life

The animals have finished helping
the beavers build a dam.
They have decided to celebrate.

Tell what you think each animal
did to get ready for the celebration.

What is your family's favorite
celebration? How do you help?

Sharing Life

Imagine the best celebration ever.

Who would be there?

What would there be to eat?

What would you wear?

What would you do?

This family is going to a special celebration.
Can you guess what it is?

Who do you think will be there?
What will everyone do at the celebration?

Why do you want to be a part of it?

In this lesson we will discover why the Mass is such a special celebration.

We Will Learn

- Jesus gives us the Mass.
- We can see and hear many things at Mass.
- The Mass is the great celebration of the Catholic Church.

169

Our Catholic Faith

■ Jesus, thank You for inviting us to Your celebration. We will come!

■ What helps to make the Mass a good celebration?

Jesus Gives Us the Mass

The friends of Jesus celebrate a special meal together. We call it the Mass. This is how the Mass began.

The night before Jesus died on the cross for us, He had a special meal with His friends. It was the last supper He had with them.

They ate, sang songs, and prayed together. They read God's word in the Bible.

Read to me from the Bible

Then Jesus took bread. He thanked God for it. He gave it to His friends.

He said, "This is My Body." Jesus took a cup of wine. He said, "This is the cup of My Blood. Do this in memory of Me."

From Luke 22:19

The **Mass** is the special celebration in which we hear God's word, remember Jesus' dying and rising, and share the Body and Blood of Christ.

The Mass Today

Jesus wanted His followers to remember His love. He wanted us to give thanks to God for all that Jesus had done.

The first Christians did what Jesus did at the Last Supper. Today Catholics also do the same thing in the celebration of the Mass.

We gather together and make the sign of the cross with the priest. We listen to God's word in the Bible. We bring gifts of bread and wine and do what Jesus told us to do. We remember that Jesus died on the cross for us and rose again. We receive Jesus' Body and Blood in Holy Communion.

- Tell what happened at the Last Supper.
- What will you do when you go to Mass?

OUR
CATHOLIC
FAITH

- Thank You, Jesus, for being with us at Mass.

- When do you like to go to Mass? Why?

We Gather to Celebrate

The Mass is the great celebration that Jesus gave us. Everything about it is special.

Jesus is with us each time we celebrate the Mass. We gather with our family and friends. We come together in our parish church on Saturday evening or on Sunday.

We celebrate Mass together as Jesus' friends. The priest leads our parish community at Mass.

We gather around a special holy table.
We call this table the altar.

A special plate and cup are used for the bread and wine.
The plate is called the paten.
The cup is called the chalice.

We pray together at Mass. Sometimes we pray out loud. Sometimes we pray in our hearts. Sometimes we pray by joining in the singing. We pray with our bodies by standing or sitting or kneeling.

Draw what you like to do best at Mass.

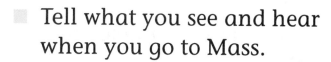 Tell what you see and hear when you go to Mass.

What do you like to do best at Mass? Share your drawings.

OUR CATHOLIC FAITH

■ Jesus, help us to listen to Your word at Mass.

■ Tell some of the things you do at Mass.

The Mass Begins

Mass is our great celebration as a parish family. Everyone has something to do at Mass. This shows we are all God's people. To begin Mass we stand together and sing.

With the priest, we make the sign of the cross. We hear the priest say, "The Lord be with you." We answer, "And also with you."

We ask God and one another for forgiveness. Then we join with the priest to tell God how wonderful He is. We get ready to listen to God's word when it is read from the Bible.

Our Greeting at Mass

Friends have special ways to greet each other. Some friends kiss or hug. Others shake hands and say, "I'm glad to see you."

Share your special way to greet your friends.

The friends of Jesus greet one another at Mass. The priest opens his arms wide to welcome us. He may say, "The Lord be with you." We answer together, "And also with you."

This greeting reminds us that we are a family of Jesus' friends. Jesus is with us at Mass. We are happy to celebrate together.

The next time you go to Mass, listen for the special greeting, "The Lord be with you." What will you answer?

Learn by heart Faith Summary

- Jesus is with us each time we celebrate the Mass.

- We all have a part to play in the Mass.

Coming To Faith

Tell about each of these ways
we celebrate at Mass.

sing   pray   listen

What can you do to join in the Mass?
Tell why you like doing this.

Practicing Faith

Jesus invites you and your family to gather
at Mass with your parish family.
Answer Jesus' invitation by finishing this
letter to Jesus.

Dear Jesus,
I will try to join with
my parish family at Mass
this weekend. I will thank
God for _____
_____
_____
_____
_____

Take a few minutes to
talk with the children
about ways they and their
families might use the
"Faith Alive" section.
Encourage them to share
My Mass Book with
their families.

REVIEW ■ TEST

Fill in the circle beside the correct answer.

1. Our special celebration in which we share the Body and Blood of Christ is _____.

○ Baptism ○ the Mass ○ the Bible

2. We gather around a holy table called the _____.

○ altar ○ chalice ○ bread

3. We listen to God's word from the _____.

○ altar ○ parish ○ Bible

4. How will you show others that you are happy to be at Mass this week?

FAITH ALIVE AT HOME AND IN THE PARISH

In this lesson your child learned that Jesus gave us the Mass. They also learned about the beginning of the Mass. It is important that first graders participate in the celebration of the Eucharist each Saturday evening or Sunday. It is the center and summit of our Catholic life. That is why we begin the lesson with a simple explanation of what it means to gather with others to worship. Help your child to understand that together we are the visible expression of the Church. Your child also began to learn the responses the assembly makes at Mass. Help him or her to learn these responses by heart.

Mass Booklet

On pages 267-270 of this book you will find *My Mass Book.* Have your child show it to you. Read it together. Encourage your child to bring it to Mass.

Dear God,
help us to love
and serve You and
other people.

Our Life

Read to me

Megan called her aunt to tell her exciting news. "Aunt Sondra, guess what! Last Sunday at Mass Dad, Mom, Jessie, and I carried up the gifts of bread and wine to the altar."

Aunt Sondra answered, "Oh, what an honor! Megan, how did you feel?"

Megan told her aunt, "At first I was afraid because everybody would be watching us. But then Dad told me that we were bringing up the gifts for everybody there. I felt very special. I hope we get to do it again."

Would you like to bring up the gifts at Mass? Why or why not?

Sharing Life

What is your favorite way to take part in the Mass? Tell about it.

What is each picture showing?
Decorate the word that tells what
we do together at Mass.
Tell why we must all join in
the celebration of Mass.

What are some things you can do?

In this lesson we will discover
more about the way we celebrate
the Mass together.

We Will Learn

- At Mass, we listen to God's word.

- Our gifts to God become
  Jesus Himself.

- We receive Jesus in Holy Communion.

Celebrate

- Let's pray together saying "The Lord be with you. And also with you."

- What do you think it means to have the Lord with us?

We Listen to God's Word

At Mass we listen to God's word. We try to be good listeners.

When the reader says, "The word of the Lord." We answer, "Thanks be to God."

Then we listen to the gospel. The gospel is the good news of Jesus.

Jesus has given us good news. The good news is that God loves us.

After the gospel, the deacon or priest says, "The gospel of the Lord." We answer, "Praise to you, Lord Jesus Christ."

The **gospel** is the good news of Jesus.

We sit and listen quietly.
The priest talks to us about
the readings from the Bible.

Then we pray a prayer that tells
what we believe. We call this our
Creed.

After this, we pray for all people.
After each prayer we answer,
"Lord, hear our prayer."

On a piece of paper, write
the name of someone you
wish to pray for at Mass.

■ Will you pray for this person
at Mass this weekend?

■ What will you say?

OUR CATHOLIC FAITH

- Take turns praying for someone. Everyone will answer, "Lord, hear our prayer."

- What gifts can you bring to God at Mass?

Our Gifts to God at Mass

Some people are asked to bring our gifts of bread and wine to the altar. This shows that we want to offer ourselves to God.

The priest prepares our gifts to be offered to God.

We pray,
"Blessed be God forever."

During the Thanksgiving Prayer, the priest says the words Jesus said at the Last Supper.

The priest takes the bread in his hands.

He prays in the name of Jesus, "This is my body which will be given up for you."

He takes the cup of wine and says, "This is the cup of my blood."

Through the words of the priest and by the power of the Holy Spirit, the bread and wine become Jesus Himself.

■ Tell what happens to our gifts of bread and wine at Mass.

■ How will you thank Jesus for being really present at Mass?

OUR CATHOLIC FAITH

- Stand and pray together: "Blessed be God forever!"

- What does it mean for Jesus to be with you always?

Holy Communion

During the Mass the bread and wine become Jesus Himself.
Jesus is really present.
Jesus Christ is our Bread of Life.
When you are ready, you can receive Jesus in Holy Communion.
When we receive the Body and Blood of Christ, we say, "Amen."

At the end of Mass, the deacon or priest says, "Go in peace to love and serve the Lord."

We answer, "Thanks be to God."

The Mass is ended.
We go in peace to love and serve God and one another.

Amen, Amen, Amen!

Amen is a wonderful prayer.
When we pray Amen we tell God,
"Yes, I believe!"

We say Amen at the end of every
prayer we learn. We also say
Amen many times at Mass.
When Communion time comes,
the priest or eucharistic minister
holds up the Host and says,
"The Body of Christ." Those who
receive answer, "Amen."

Our Amen means that we believe
Jesus is with us in Holy Communion.

Make up an Amen prayer.
Tell Jesus something you
believe about Him.

†Jesus, I believe

_____

- -

_____ Amen!

Take turns praying your prayer.

Learn by heart Faith Summary

- We listen to God's word at Mass.
- Our gifts to God become Jesus, whom
  we receive in Holy Communion.

COMING TO FAITH

What happens to our gifts of bread and wine at Mass?

Tell about your favorite part of the Mass.

Why is it your favorite?

PRACTICING FAITH

Look at the pictures of the Mass in this lesson. Tell what is happening in each picture.

Put yourself in one of the pictures. Tell what you will do to take part next time you go to Mass.

Talk to the children about ways they and their families might use the "Faith Alive" section. Encourage the children to ask someone at home to go over and practice the Mass responses with them.

REVIEW ■ TEST

Circle the correct response.

1. When the reader says "The word of the Lord," we say _____.

"Amen"   "Thanks be to God"

2. After each of the prayers for all people, we say _____.

"Lord, hear our prayer"   "Alleluia"

3. When we hear "The gospel of the Lord," we say _____.

"Praise to you, Lord Jesus Christ"   "Amen"

4. Tell one way you will love and serve God this week.

FAITH ALIVE AT HOME AND IN THE PARISH

In this lesson your child deepened his or her understanding of the Mass and the real presence of Jesus in the Eucharist. Help your child to appreciate that Jesus is truly present to us in the Liturgy of the Word, preparing us for union with Him in the Liturgy of the Eucharist. Point out that the bread and wine become the Body and Blood of Christ. This happens through the words and actions of the priest and by the power of the Holy Spirit.

Renewed by the Eucharist, the Body and Blood of Christ, we are called to be "bread of life" for others—especially the poor and the suffering.

Responding at Mass
Practice the Mass responses with your child. Point them out in *My Mass Book* and encourage your child to participate as fully as possible at Mass.

Jesus, help me
spend quiet
prayer time
with You.

Our Life

Read to me
Shelly Turtle had many friends in the bayou.
She loved to talk with them and help them.

One morning, she was sitting in the sun.
Her friends Gator and Froggie wanted
her to play. But Shelly said, "Not right now!
I need some quiet time. I'm just going
to go inside, relax, and think."

Gator asked, "How about this afternoon?"
Shelly answered, "That would be great!
See you later, Gator!"

Do you sometimes like to take
time out for quiet time alone?
When do you do this?

Sharing Life

Do you like to talk to God
during quiet time? Why?

How does it feel to talk to God?
Tell how this helps you.

Imagine that you and Jesus are sitting together right now—just the two of you.

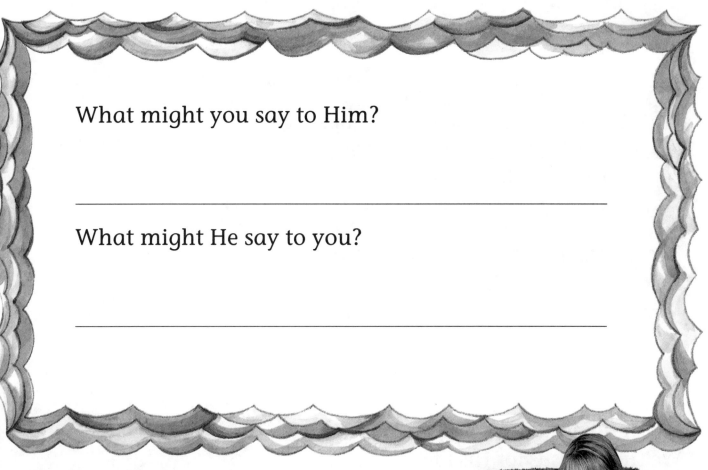

What might you say to Him?

_____

What might He say to you?

_____

Now be very still with Jesus. Sometimes good friends do not need any words at all.

In this lesson we will discover that Lent is a great time to grow closer to Jesus.

We Will Learn

- We need quiet time to talk to Jesus.

- Jesus wants us to love one another as He loves us.

189

Jesus teaches us that we need quiet time.
He spent quiet time praying to God.
He went to the desert and hills
to talk and listen to God.

Lent is a special time to pray and to grow
in love for Jesus. We talk and listen to
Jesus, our best friend, in quiet time.
We remember Jesus died for us.
We remember Jesus rose from the dead
to give us new life.
We thank Jesus for all He did for us.
We thank Jesus for His love.
We tell Jesus how much we want to
grow in love for Him.
We ask Jesus to help us share His love
with others, especially those in need.

We remember that Jesus said, "Love one
another, just as I love you."

From John 15:12

COMING TO FAITH

Think of ways you can take time to grow as a friend of Jesus. Here is one way to pray in your heart during Lent.

Be still like a turtle inside its shell. If you want to, close your eyes. Feel the love of Jesus all around you. Imagine you hear Jesus say, "You are My friend. Talk to Me."

✝ Jesus, I want to tell You …
Jesus, I want to thank You …
Jesus, I was wondering …
Jesus, help me to grow in …
Jesus, help me to share …

191

Practicing Faith

Imagine you hear Jesus say, "Go, My friend. Help others to grow in their love for Me."

How will you do this during Lent? The pictures on this page may help.

Make signs for your door to help you tell others how you are spending time — alone or with others — in Lent.

Talk to the children about ways they and their families might use the "Faith Alive" section. Encourage the children to share quiet prayer time with their families during Lent.

REVIEW ■ TEST

Put an x in the box next to each sentence that tells what we are expected to do during Lent.

1. ☐ We remember Jesus died for us.

2. ☐ We get ready for Christmas.

3. ☐ We think of ways to share with others.

4. ☐ We thank Jesus for all He did for us.

5. Tell one thing you will do for Jesus this Lent.

FAITH ALIVE AT HOME AND IN THE PARISH

In this lesson your child was introduced to the liturgical season of Lent as a special time for prayer and good works. Lent is a season of forty days that begins on Ash Wednesday. During this time Catholics renew their efforts to live their Baptism. They also fast and abstain on certain days. We are encouraged to do works of mercy and justice and to prepare ourselves to celebrate the high point of the Church year—the Easter Triduum.

Learn by heart **Faith Summary**

- Lent is a special time to grow in love for Jesus.

- We remember that Jesus died for us and rose from the dead.

21 Easter

Alleluia, Jesus!
We have good
news to tell!

OUR LIFE

What words do you say
when you are excited or very happy?

How do they help you tell
others how you feel?

SHARING LIFE

Celebrate and share Easter
good news.

Act out the prayer words.

† God, Your world says Alleluia!
Birds fly from tree to tree
and chirp in early morning.
Frogs hop near the pond
and croak. Butterflies quietly
flutter their wings.

Bees dance upon the flowers
opening in sunlight.
They buzz happily.

And I jump for joy and say,
"Alleluia! We celebrate Jesus'
new life."

HOSANNA

Another word we say to praise God is "Hosanna."
With this word, we thank God for saving us.
Think of a time during Mass when you hear the word Hosanna.

Hosanna is also a way to say "Welcome." Think of a way you can say welcome to Jesus. Write this message to Jesus on a postcard.

Pray:

✝Blessed is he who comes in the name of the Lord, Hosanna in the highest!

In this lesson we will hear again the good news of Easter.

We Will Learn

- Jesus rose from the dead.
- We celebrate Jesus' new life at Easter.
- Jesus shares His new life with us.

An Easter Play

Narrator: Mary Magdalene was crying outside of Jesus' tomb because Jesus' body was not there. A young man by the tomb said to Mary:

Angel: Why are you crying?

Mary: They have taken Jesus away. I do not know where they have put Him.

Narrator: When Mary said this, she saw Jesus standing by her, but she did not know that it was Jesus.

Jesus: Why are you crying? Who are you looking for?

Narrator: Mary thought at first that Jesus was the gardener.

Mary: If you took Jesus away, tell me where you have put Him. I will go and get Him.

Narrator: Then Jesus said her name.

Jesus: Mary!

Narrator: Mary turned toward Jesus. She knew who it was. She said:

Mary: Teacher!

Jesus: Go tell My friends that I am going back to My Father.

Narrator: Mary went back to Jesus' friends and told them that she had seen Jesus. He was alive!

From John 20:11–18

Coming To Faith

What did you learn from the story of Mary Magdalene at the tomb?

On Easter we show how happy
we are that Jesus is alive.
He shares His new life with us.
We pray and sing Alleluia.

Sing this happy Alleluia song.
(To the tune of "Skip to My Lou")

♫ Alle! Alleluia!
Alle! Alleluia!
Alle! Alleluia!
Jesus gives us new life! ♫

197

PRACTICING FAITH

Make an Easter Good News banner.
Share the banner with your family.
How will you celebrate the good news
of Easter at home and in your parish?

Take a few minutes to talk with the
children about ways they and their
families might use the "Faith Alive"
section. Encourage them to share signs
of new life with their families.

REVIEW ■ TEST

Put the Easter story in order by numbering the sentences 1 through 5.

☐ Jesus said her name. "Mary!"

☐ Mary saw Jesus but thought He was the gardener.

☐ Mary Magdalene could not find Jesus' body in the tomb.

☐ The angel said, "Why are you crying?"

☐ Jesus said, "Go tell My friends that I am going back to My Father."

FAITH ALIVE AT HOME AND IN THE PARISH

In this lesson your child learned that after Jesus died He rose to new life. It is this new life that He shares with us. We celebrate the resurrection of Jesus Christ every Sunday. We celebrate it most solemnly on Easter Sunday itself. It is the day of Jesus' final victory for us over death and sin. It is the feast of Christian hope—we are assured in the resurrection of Christ that we, too, will rise to new life. Easter calls Christians to a renewed and living faith—a faith that reaches out to the poor, the abandoned, and the despairing so that they may know the hope won for us by Christ.

Learn by heart **Faith Summary**

- Jesus rose from the dead on Easter.

- Jesus gives us new life.

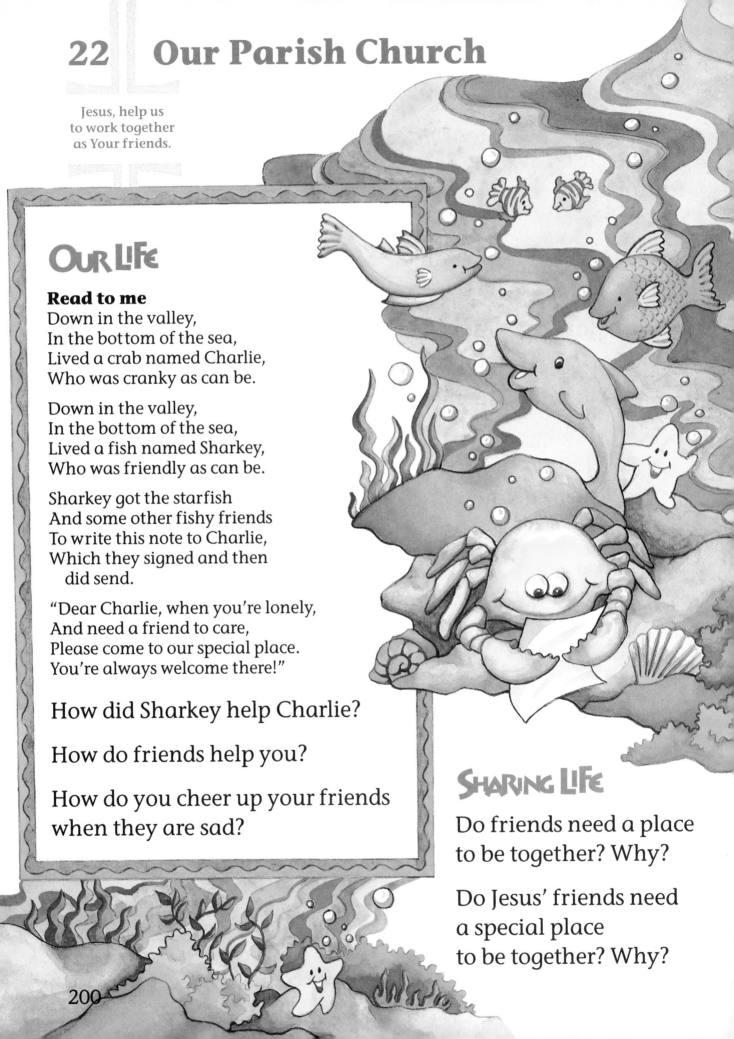

Jesus, help us
to work together
as Your friends.

Our Life

Read to me
Down in the valley,
In the bottom of the sea,
Lived a crab named Charlie,
Who was cranky as can be.

Down in the valley,
In the bottom of the sea,
Lived a fish named Sharkey,
Who was friendly as can be.

Sharkey got the starfish
And some other fishy friends
To write this note to Charlie,
Which they signed and then
    did send.

"Dear Charlie, when you're lonely,
And need a friend to care,
Please come to our special place.
You're always welcome there!"

How did Sharkey help Charlie?

How do friends help you?

How do you cheer up your friends
when they are sad?

Sharing Life

Do friends need a place
to be together? Why?

Do Jesus' friends need
a special place
to be together? Why?

Name your favorite place to be with your friends.

Imagine you and your friends are in your special place.
What are you doing together?
How do you feel?

Draw a face on the starfish to show how you feel.

In this lesson we will discover that our parish is a special place where Jesus' friends gather together.

We Will Learn

- Our parish is a special place.

- Everyone in our parish is important.

- We belong to the Catholic Church.

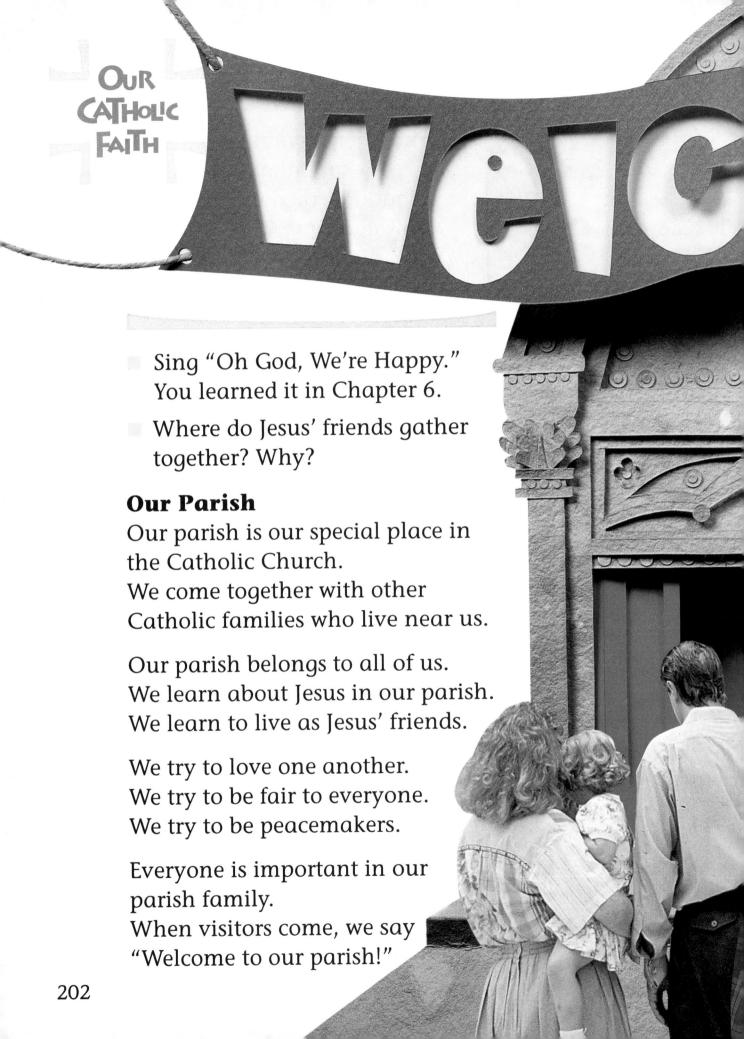

■ Sing "Oh God, We're Happy."
You learned it in Chapter 6.

■ Where do Jesus' friends gather
together? Why?

Our Parish

Our parish is our special place in
the Catholic Church.
We come together with other
Catholic families who live near us.

Our parish belongs to all of us.
We learn about Jesus in our parish.
We learn to live as Jesus' friends.

We try to love one another.
We try to be fair to everyone.
We try to be peacemakers.

Everyone is important in our
parish family.
When visitors come, we say
"Welcome to our parish!"

The **parish** is our special place in the Catholic Church.

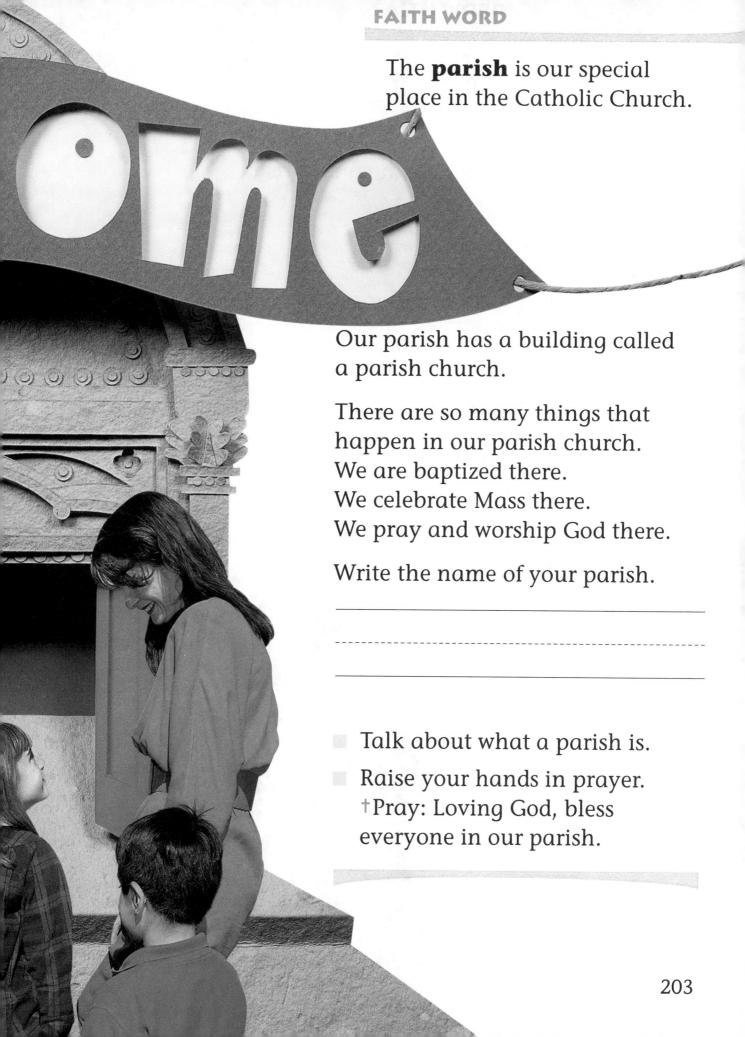

Our parish has a building called a parish church.

There are so many things that happen in our parish church.
We are baptized there.
We celebrate Mass there.
We pray and worship God there.

Write the name of your parish.

_____

- -

_____

Talk about what a parish is.

Raise your hands in prayer.
†Pray: Loving God, bless everyone in our parish.

203

OUR
CATHOLIC
FAITH

■ Jesus, thank You for our parish family.

■ Tell some things you can do in your parish.

We All Help Our Parish

Everyone in our parish is important.
We all have something special to do.

Many people make up our parish family.
There are young people, old people, families, and friends.

Some people help us to celebrate the Mass.

Some people read God's word to us.

Some of them give us Holy Communion.

Some people in our parish help the poor, the sick, and the lonely.
Some people teach us about God.
Some people work for peace.

The priest in our parish brings us all together.
He leads us as we worship God at Mass.
He helps us to care for one another.

Write the name of a priest in your parish. Call him by name when you see him.

Hello, Father

_____

- -

_____

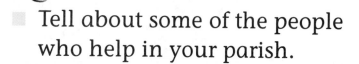

■ Tell about some of the people who help in your parish.

■ What will you do in your parish this week?

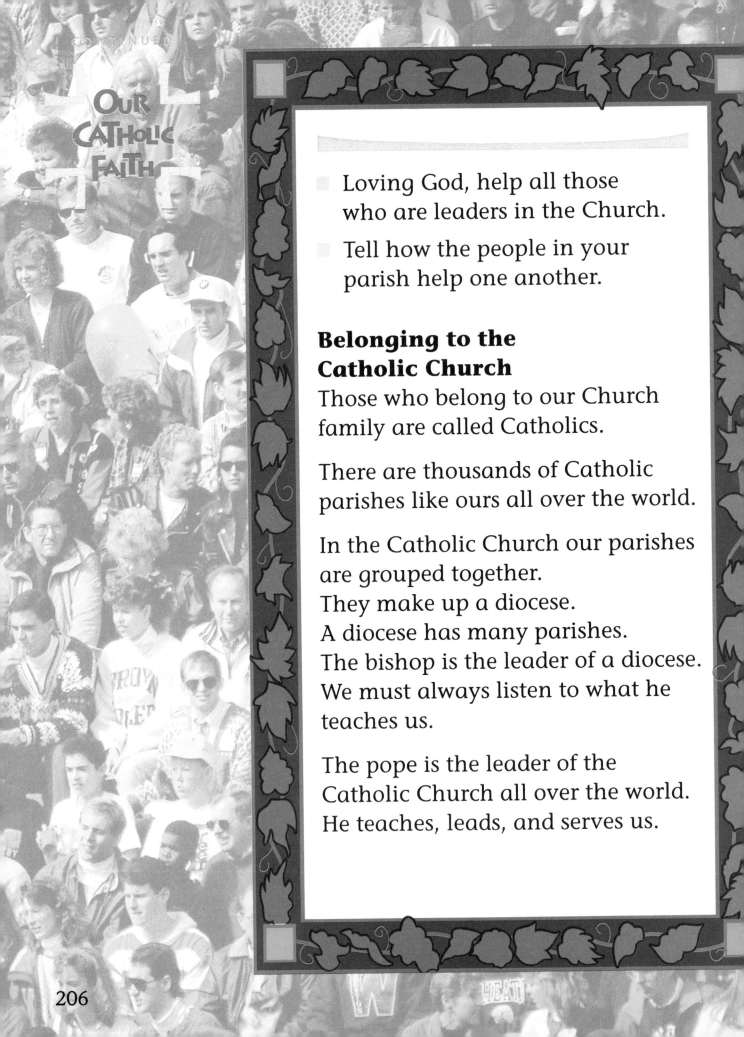

- Loving God, help all those who are leaders in the Church.

- Tell how the people in your parish help one another.

Belonging to the Catholic Church

Those who belong to our Church family are called Catholics.

There are thousands of Catholic parishes like ours all over the world.

In the Catholic Church our parishes are grouped together.
They make up a diocese.
A diocese has many parishes.
The bishop is the leader of a diocese.
We must always listen to what he teaches us.

The pope is the leader of the Catholic Church all over the world.
He teaches, leads, and serves us.

A Visit to Our Parish Church

Our parish church belongs to all of us. It is filled with things that remind us of God's love for us.

Look at the pictures of things we see in our parish church. What does each one tell us about God's love for us?

Ask someone in your family to take you to church for a visit. Talk about the things you see. Say a prayer together to thank God for loving you so much.

Learn by heart **Faith Summary**

- Our parish is our special place in the Catholic Church.

- Everyone helps in our parish.

207

Coming To Faith

Tell three ways people help
one another in your parish.

Some people in our parish
are sick. They cannot go outside.
Let's help someone.
Send them a special surprise.

Trace the fish and cut it out. Color the fish.
Join it with others to make an underwater scene.
Write on your picture, "We love you!"

Ask your catechist or pastor
to bring your scene to someone
in your parish who is sick.

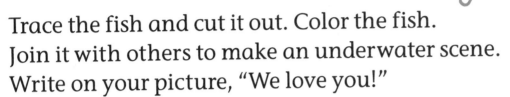

We love you.

Practicing Faith

Name one way you would like
to help in your parish this week.

Invite one of your friends to visit your
parish church.

Talk to the children
about ways they and
their families might use
the "Faith Alive" section.
Then pray the prayer for
your parish on page 203
as a closing faith
response.

REVIEW ■ TEST

Circle the correct answer.

1. Our special place in the Catholic Church is the _____.

      diocese   parish

2. Our parish family comes together in a building called the _____.

      diocese   parish church

3. We are _____ in our parish church.

      baptized   born

4. All those who belong to our Church are called _____.

      Catholics   priests

5. What can you tell a friend about your parish?

23 Our Catholic Church

OUR LIFE

Here is a poem about the wind.
Make up your own actions.

Who has seen the wind?
Neither I nor you.
But when the leaves
    hang trembling,
The wind is passing through.

Who has seen the wind?
Neither you nor I.
But when the leaves
    bow down their heads,
The wind is passing by.

Christina G. Rossetti

We do not see the wind.
How do you know that the wind is blowing?

We do not see God.
How do we know that God is with us?

SHARING LIFE

How does knowing God is with you
make you feel?
Tell Him in the quiet of your heart.

God is with

Finish the message on the kite. Decorate the kite with things that help you know God is with you.

Share the message on your kite with a friend.

Imagine you are the kite floating in the sky. Pray slowly,

† God, be with me.
God, be with others.
God, be with us always.

In this lesson we will discover how Catholics show that God is with us always.

We Will Learn

- Catholics pray to God.
- Catholics celebrate the sacraments.
- The Catholic Church helps us to be holy.

OUR CATHOLIC FAITH

Pray the Our Father together (page 109).

When do you pray to God? How?

Catholics Pray

All around the world, Catholics pray to God.

There are prayers we say together and prayers we say alone.

Sometimes we pray in our own words.
We talk to God as a friend.
Sometimes we sing our prayers.

- We can praise God, who made us.

- We can tell Him we are sorry for something we have done wrong.

- We can ask God's help for all people.

- We can ask His help for our own needs.

- We can thank God for His love and care.

Sometimes we pray the prayer that Jesus taught us, the Our Father.

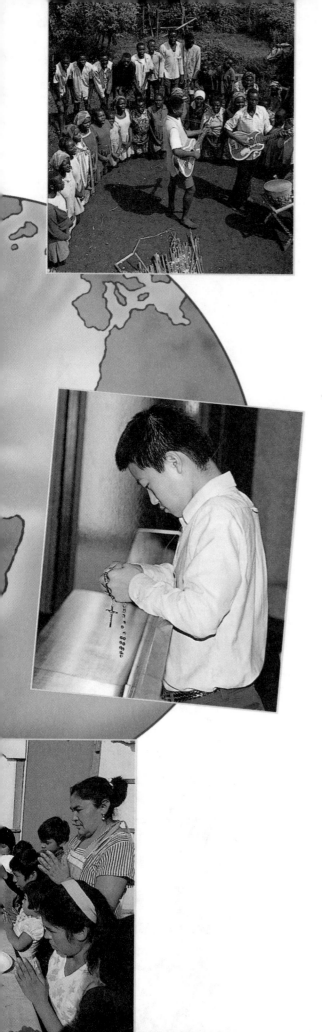

Catholics have a special love
for Mary.
She is the mother of Jesus and our
mother, too.

We ask Mary to pray to God for us.
Here is a beautiful prayer to Mary
that Catholics pray.
It is called the Hail Mary.

Learn this prayer to Mary
by heart.

† Hail Mary, full of grace,
the Lord is with you;
blessed are you among women,
and blessed is the fruit
of your womb, Jesus.
Holy Mary, Mother of God,
pray for us sinners
now and at the hour of our death.
Amen.

- Why do Catholics pray to
  Mary?

- Pray the Hail Mary often until
  everyone knows it well.

Our Catholic Faith

- Pray the Hail Mary together again.
- Tell about your favorite prayer.

Our Church Celebrates

Jesus gave His Church special signs that God is with us. They are called sacraments. In the sacraments, our Church does what Jesus did to show God's love and care for everyone.

Jesus welcomed all people into His community of friends. In the sacrament of Baptism, our Church welcomes all people into our Church community.

Jesus promised to send the Holy Spirit to be our Helper. In the sacrament of Confirmation, the Holy Spirit comes to us in a special way.

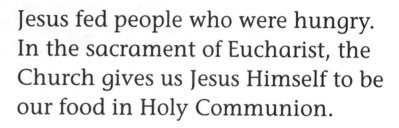

To **worship** is to give honor and praise to God.

Jesus fed people who were hungry. In the sacrament of Eucharist, the Church gives us Jesus Himself to be our food in Holy Communion.

Jesus forgave people their sins. In the sacrament of Reconciliation, the Church brings us God's forgiveness and mercy.

Catholics all over the world celebrate the sacraments. When we celebrate the sacraments, we worship God together.

- Explain why we worship God.
- Have you celebrated one of the sacraments? Tell about it.

OUR CATHOLIC FAITH

- Jesus, teach us and help us to live as You want us to live.

- What sacraments can you name?

Being Holy

We are Jesus' friends, the Church.
The Church helps us to be holy.
To be holy means to belong to God
and to live as Jesus taught us.

This is how we become holy.
We talk to God.
We celebrate the sacraments.
We live as friends of Jesus.
We tell others about God our Father.

In the Bible we read, "You are called to be a holy people. You belong to God. You are God's own people."

From 1 Peter 2:9–10

216

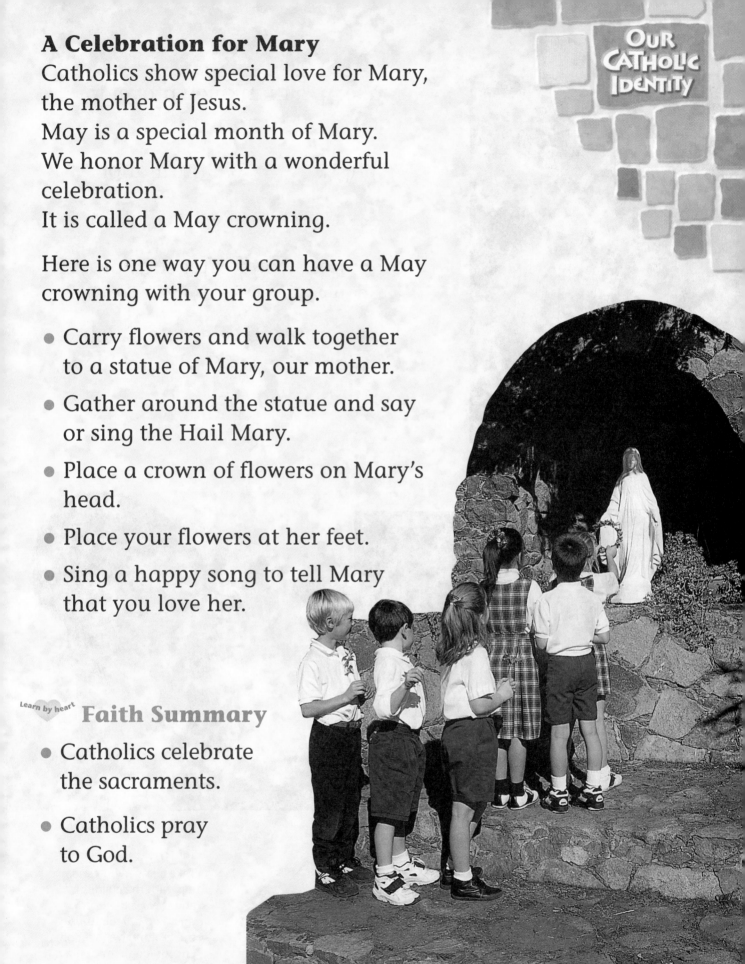

A Celebration for Mary

Catholics show special love for Mary, the mother of Jesus.
May is a special month of Mary.
We honor Mary with a wonderful celebration.
It is called a May crowning.

Here is one way you can have a May crowning with your group.

- Carry flowers and walk together to a statue of Mary, our mother.

- Gather around the statue and say or sing the Hail Mary.

- Place a crown of flowers on Mary's head.

- Place your flowers at her feet.

- Sing a happy song to tell Mary that you love her.

Learn by heart **Faith Summary**

- Catholics celebrate the sacraments.

- Catholics pray to God.

COMING TO FAITH

Make up a thank-you prayer for each of the sacraments.

Baptism   Confirmation

Eucharist   Reconciliation

Sing these words after each prayer.
(To the tune of "Michael, Row the Boat")

♫ Let us pray and celebrate, Alleluia,
Gifts and signs of God's great love,
Alleluia. ♫

PRACTICING FAITH

Circle ways that you will celebrate and pray. Tell about them.

Gather in a circle and hold hands. Pray the Hail Mary together.

Take a few minutes to talk with the children about ways they and their families might use the "Faith Alive" section. Encourage them to pray the Hail Mary with someone at home each night this week and to learn it by heart.

REVIEW ▪ TEST

Fill in the circle beside the correct answer.

1. We are welcomed into the Church in the sacrament
of _____.

   ◯ the Eucharist   ◯ Confirmation   ◯ Baptism

2. The Holy Spirit comes in a special way in the sacrament
of _____.

   ◯ Baptism   ◯ Confirmation   ◯ the Eucharist

3. Jesus gives us Himself in _____.

   ◯ the Eucharist   ◯ Confirmation   ◯ Baptism

4. The special prayer we say to the mother of Jesus
is the _____.

   ◯ Our Father   ◯ Sign of the Cross   ◯ Hail Mary

5. Tell some ways you can pray.

FAITH ALIVE ▪ AT HOME AND IN THE PARISH

This week your child learned that the Catholic Church is a community of prayer. It is also a worshiping community that celebrates the sacraments together. When we take part often, knowingly, and actively in the Church's life of prayer and worship, we experience ourselves as a priestly people. This is an aspect of our baptismal commitment to "proclaim the wonderful acts of God, who called us out of darkness into God's own marvelous light" (from 1 Peter 2:9).

Celebrating the sacraments and praying often as a family are wonderful ways to help our children grow strong in their Catholic faith and in their love of God and neighbor.

Ways to Pray

Your child has circled, on page 218, ways in which he or she will pray this week. Help your child find a time and place for prayer. An appropriate time for this is before your child goes to sleep at night.

Grace at Meals

Saying grace before and after meals is a wonderful custom. If your family does not usually say grace, you might want to begin the practice. The traditional grace prayers at meals are on page 276. Occasionally you might encourage family members to take turns offering spontaneous meal prayers.

24   The Church Helps People

OUR LIFE

Look at each picture.
Tell what is happening.

Which children are being fair?
Which child is being unfair?

Have you ever been treated unfairly?
How did you feel?

Do you ever treat others unfairly?
How?

SHARING LIFE

What does it mean to be unfair to someone?

Why are we sometimes unfair to others?

Why do you think Jesus wants us to be fair
to everyone?

Think about what our world would be like if we were all fair to one another.

Work with a partner to make a flag for the world.

On the back of the flag, write a wish for the world.

Share your flag with the group. Take turns praying your wishes.

In this lesson we will discover how the Church helps us to be fair to everyone.

We Will Learn

- The Church helps us to be fair to others.

- The Church helps us to know and live what Jesus taught.

- With our Church community, we share the good news of Jesus with others.

OUR CATHOLIC FAITH

- Take turns telling God your wishes for the world.

- How does God want you to treat other people?

The Church Helps People

The Catholic Church helps people by teaching us how to be fair. The Church helps us to know what Jesus taught.

Here is a story Jesus told about being fair.

Read to me from the Bible

Once there was a servant who owed the king a lot of money. He could not pay what he owed. He begged the king, "Please give me more time to pay what I owe you." The king felt sorry for his servant. He said, "You do not have to pay me back any money."

The servant was very happy. Then he went to see a man who owed him a little money. The man begged, "Please give me more time to pay what I owe you." The servant said, "No! You must pay me now!"

The king was very angry at the way his servant treated the man. He said, "You should have been fair to the man, just as I was fair to you."
From Matthew 18:22–34

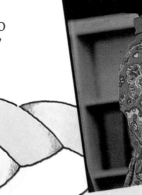

What do you learn from this story?

Being fair means treating people the way we want them to treat us.

It also means caring for people who need our help, especially the poor.

Jesus teaches us that it does not matter how young or old a person is. It does not matter what color skin a person has. God wants us to be fair to everyone.

When we are fair, we show people that God loves everyone.

- Why was the king in the story angry with his servant?

- Tell some ways that you can be fair.

PEACE

OUR CATHOLIC FAITH

- Help us, God, to be fair to everyone.

- Tell some ways that you can be a peacemaker.

We Bring Peace to Others

When we are fair to one another, we help to make peace.

Peace is a wonderful gift of God. Peace means not fighting. Peace means not hurting others. Peace means being quiet inside ourselves.

Jesus gives us His gift of peace. Jesus said, "My peace is My gift to you."

From John 14:27

In the Church we try to live in peace with one another. Jesus wants us to be peacemakers in our world.

Jesus said,
"Happy are the peacemakers. They will be called children of God."

From Matthew 5:9

Draw a picture of someone being a peacemaker.

- What did Jesus say about peacemakers?
- What will you do to be a peacemaker today?

■ Help us, God, to be peacemakers.

■ What good news of Jesus can
you share?

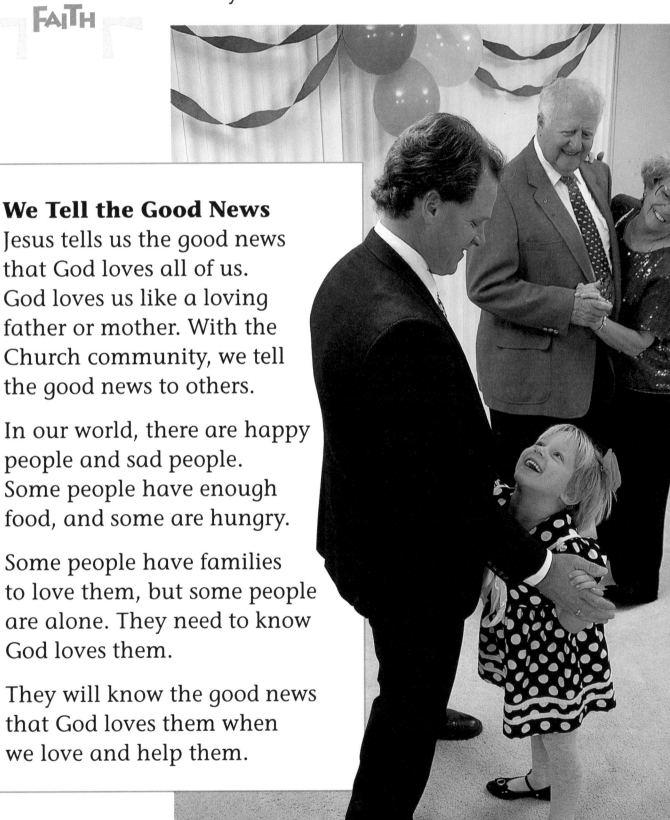

We Tell the Good News

Jesus tells us the good news
that God loves all of us.
God loves us like a loving
father or mother. With the
Church community, we tell
the good news to others.

In our world, there are happy
people and sad people.
Some people have enough
food, and some are hungry.

Some people have families
to love them, but some people
are alone. They need to know
God loves them.

They will know the good news
that God loves them when
we love and help them.

Sharing Peace

During Mass we can show that we want to be peacemakers, too.

Just before we receive Jesus in Holy Communion, we share a sign of peace with those around us.

Let us share a sign of peace now. Shake hands with one another and say, "The peace of Christ be with you."

Color the banner and then say this prayer for peacemakers.

† Let Jesus' peace be with me.

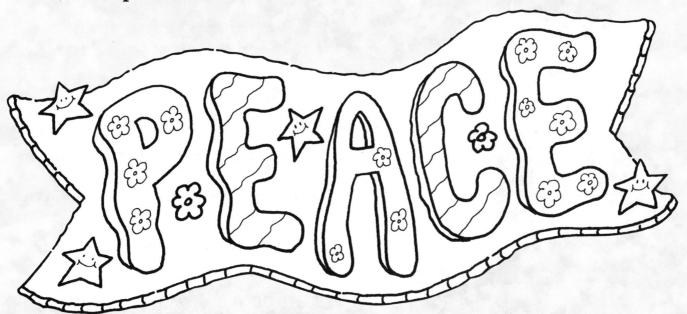

Learn by heart **Faith Summary**

- Catholics try to treat others fairly and live in peace.

- Jesus wants us to be peacemakers.

COMING TO FAITH

Be a peace partner!
Pretend you are Jesus.
How can you help the
children in each picture
act fairly and make peace?

What would Jesus say?

What would Jesus do?

PRACTICING FAITH

Jesus wants us to be fair
and to keep peace in our hearts.

Be still. Pray slowly.

† Jesus, You give me peace.
(Breathe in. Breathe out.)
May Your peace be with me always.
(Breathe in. Breathe out.)
Jesus, help me bring
Your peace to others.
This week, help me to be fair to . . .
(Name someone in your heart.)
Help me to be at peace with . . .
(Name someone in your heart.)

Take a few minutes to talk to the
children about ways they and their
families might use the "Faith Alive"
section. Encourage them to find ways
to share the peace of Christ this week.

REVIEW ■ TEST

Circle **Yes** or **No**.
If you are not sure, circle **?**.

1. Being fair means treating people
   any way we want.   **Yes**   **No**   **?**

2. Being fair means showing people
   that God loves everyone.   **Yes**   **No**   **?**

3. God wants us to be fair to everyone.   **Yes**   **No**   **?**

4. Jesus gives us His gift of peace.   **Yes**   **No**   **?**

5. Tell how you will be a peacemaker.

FAITH ALIVE AT HOME AND IN THE PARISH

The Church's teaching on justice and peace is soundly rooted in the Old and New Testaments. That the covenant demands justice is a constant theme of the prophets.

Jesus Christ is the Son of God and our Savior. He came to set us free from sin. Through Him, we have life in all its fullness and know God as our Father.

From the proclamation of Jesus' birth to His farewell at the Last Supper, His mission brought justice and peace for all people. The Catholic Church clearly teaches that our Christian faith gives us serious social responsibilities. All of us are called to work for God's kingdom of justice and peace in the world. We follow the example of Jesus, who had compassion for all people.

Children need to be given opportunities to practice fairness and forgiveness in their daily lives. The family is the most important place for developing the virtues of justice, mercy, and peace.

†Quiet Time

Spend time in quiet reflection, praying with your child about his or her worries. Encourage your child to place his or her worries in Jesus' hands and to ask Jesus for courage. Invite your child to show you the quiet prayer he or she learned this week (see page 228).

229

25 God Forgives Us

Our Life

Read to me
I was very angry.
My face turned red,
When I heard
What my sister said.

She started to fight
In the middle of the game.
I got upset,
And called a name.

Mom told us both
To forgive and forget,
But I don't think
We can do that yet.

Has something like this
Ever happened to you?
Tell about it.
What did you do?

Sharing Life

Tell how you feel when you forgive someone.

Tell how you feel when someone forgives you.

Does God want us to forgive other people? Why?

Why do we sometimes need to ask God to forgive us?

230

Draw a big flower box. On it print "My Forgiveness Box."

Add a flower to the box each time you forgive someone. Look at your forgiveness garden each day to see how you are growing as a forgiving person.

Ask God to help you to forgive and to ask for forgiveness, too.

In this lesson we will discover that God always loves us and forgives us.

We Will Learn

- Sometimes we need to say we are sorry.
- God always forgives us if we are sorry.
- The Church forgives us in God's name.

MY FORGIVENESS BOX

Pray the Morning Offering
on page 275.

When do we need to say,
"I am sorry"?

Being Sorry

We belong to God.
We are baptized.
We are God's children.
We know that God wants us
to love Him, love others,
and love ourselves.

When we do something we should
not do, we need to show we are
sorry. There are lots of ways to
tell others, "I am sorry."

We can do something nice for them.
We can give a hug. We can shake
hands. We can say what is in our
hearts.

We also need to tell God that
we are sorry.

Draw a picture that shows how you like to say you are sorry.

When do you need to tell God you are sorry?

How will you show God and others you are sorry?

OUR CATHOLIC FAITH

■ Help us, Jesus, to say "I am sorry."

■ What do you think God does when we are sorry?

God Forgives Us

God always loves us, no matter what we do. God always forgives us if we are sorry. In the Bible Jesus told this story to teach us that God always forgives.

Read to me from the Bible

Once there was a young man who decided to take his money and leave his father's home. For a while he had a lot of fun doing just what he wanted to do. He had new friends. But when all his money was gone, all his friends left him. He had no place to stay and nothing to eat. He knew he had done wrong. He decided to go back home and tell his father how sorry he was.

His father was so happy to see him! He forgave his son and had a party to welcome him home.

From Luke 15:11–24

Jesus tells us that God will always forgive us, just like the father in the story.

Use the picture to tell the story of the forgiving father in your own words.

- Imagine the party the father gave to welcome his son. What was it like?

- How do you know that God will always forgive us?

OUR CATHOLIC FAITH

- Help me, O God, to forgive others as You forgive me.

- Tell how you feel when you are forgiven.

The Church Forgives

In the Catholic Church we have a special way to celebrate that God forgives us. It is called the the sacrament of Reconciliation. In this sacrament, we pray and thank God for loving us and forgiving us.

We meet with the priest.
We tell God that we are sorry for our sins. The priest forgives us in God's name. How wonderful it is to know that God forgives us.

When you are ready, you will be able to celebrate the sacrament of Reconciliation.

We Think About Our Day

How do you know if you are growing as a child of God? Catholics have a special way to think about this.

Find a quiet place to think about the things you did today.

- Did you pray to God?
- Did you play fair?
- Did you forgive someone?
- Did you obey the people who take care of you?
- Did you take care of yourself by eating good food?
- Were you kind to someone in need?

Thank God for the good things you did today. Tell God you are sorry for the things you may have done that are wrong. Ask God to help you find ways to do better tomorrow.

Learn by heart **Faith Summary**

- God always forgives us if we are sorry.

- The priest forgives us in God's name.

COMING TO FAITH

Tell the Bible story
about the son who left home.
Follow the path that leads him
back home to his father.
Tell what the father said
when he saw his son.

Does God always forgive us
when we are sorry?
Why?

PRACTICING FAITH

Do you need to ask someone to forgive
you? What will you say?

Is there someone you would like to
forgive? What will you say?

Turn to page 109. Find the words in the
Our Father that tell us about forgiveness.
Pray the Our Father together.

Take a few minutes to talk with the
children about ways they and their
families might share the "Faith Alive"
section. Encourage them to pray
the Our Father with someone at
home and to talk about what it
means to say "as we forgive those
who trespass against us."

REVIEW ■ TEST

Fill in the circle beside the correct answer.

1. We celebrate God's forgiveness in the sacrament of _____ .

    ○ Baptism   ○ Eucharist   ○ Reconciliation

2. God says this is what we must do for God, others, and ourselves.

    ○ love   ○ play   ○ work

3. When we do what is wrong God forgives us if we _____ .

    ○ are sorry   ○ keep quiet   ○ know we are wrong

4. The priest forgives us in the name of _____ .

    ○ himself   ○ God   ○ Mary

5. What will you say to God for forgiving you?

FAITH ALIVE AT HOME AND IN THE PARISH

In this lesson your child has been given a basic understanding of forgiveness and was introduced to the sacrament of Reconciliation. In this sacrament the Church continues Jesus' ministry of forgiving sinners. Such forgiveness means not just telling God we are sorry, but also seeking ways of repairing any harm done to those we have hurt. The Catechism of the Catholic Church reiterates this important aspect of reconciliation. This lesson also helps your child understand the need for each of us to forgive others.

Forgiving and Being Forgiven

Talk with your child to build an understanding of what it means to say both "I am sorry" and "I forgive you." Help him or her to see that it is necessary to show how you are sorry and how you forgive. Think of ways you can model both of these attitudes for your child this week.

239

26　Living With God Forever

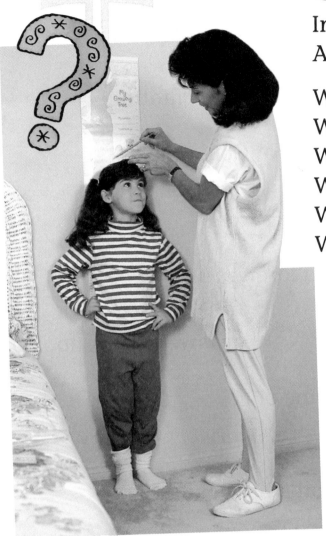

Our Life

Imagine you are in second grade.
Ask yourself these questions.

Will I look the same as I do today?
Will I be taller than I am now?
Will I have the same number of teeth?
Will I be in the same classroom?
Will I have the same teacher?
Will I like to do the same things?

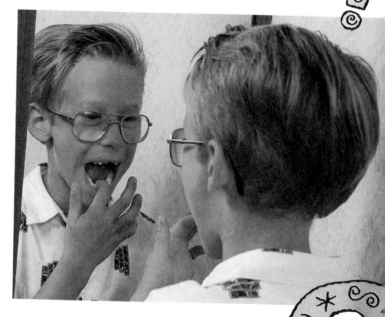

Sharing Life

What do you think will stay the same about you? Why?

What do you think will be different? Why?

Does anything stay the same forever?

What do you think lasts forever?

Cut out a big paper heart.
On it, draw or write what you think lasts forever.

Join your heart with the other hearts on a long ribbon. Then gather in a circle and hold the ribbon.

Pray together,
† God, as we grow and change,
One thing will stay the same.
You will always love us
And know us each by name.

In this lesson we will discover that God's love for us will last forever.

☀ We Will Learn

- Jesus wants us to be with Him forever.
- God's love for us will never end.
- Jesus will be with us during the summer.

OUR CATHOLIC FAITH

- Pray the prayer you prayed on page 241.

- How do you think Jesus feels about children?

We Can Be with God Forever

This Bible story shows us how much Jesus loves us and wants us to be with God forever.

Read to me from the Bible

Once Jesus had been teaching the people all day, and He was very tired.

Some people brought their children to see Jesus. The friends of Jesus told them to go away and not to bother Jesus.

Jesus was angry at this. He said to His friends, "Let the children come to Me. The kingdom of God belongs to them."

Then Jesus took the children in His arms and blessed them.

From Mark 10:13–16

Let the children

We are God's own children and friends of Jesus. If we live as children of God as Jesus showed us, we will be happy with Him forever in heaven.

- Imagine you are one of the children who came to Jesus. What will you say to Him?
- Thank You, Jesus, for blessing me.

come to me.

Good

■ Tell how you would feel if Jesus put His arms around you and blessed you.

■ Tell some of the favorite things you learned this year in religion class.

God's Love Lasts Forever

Here is some of the good news we learned this year.

Remembering these things will help us live as children of God and friends of Jesus.

- Jesus showed us how to love God, one another, and ourselves.
- Jesus taught us how to be fair and to live in peace.
- Jesus taught us to help people in need.
- God made our world.
- God made us and loves us.

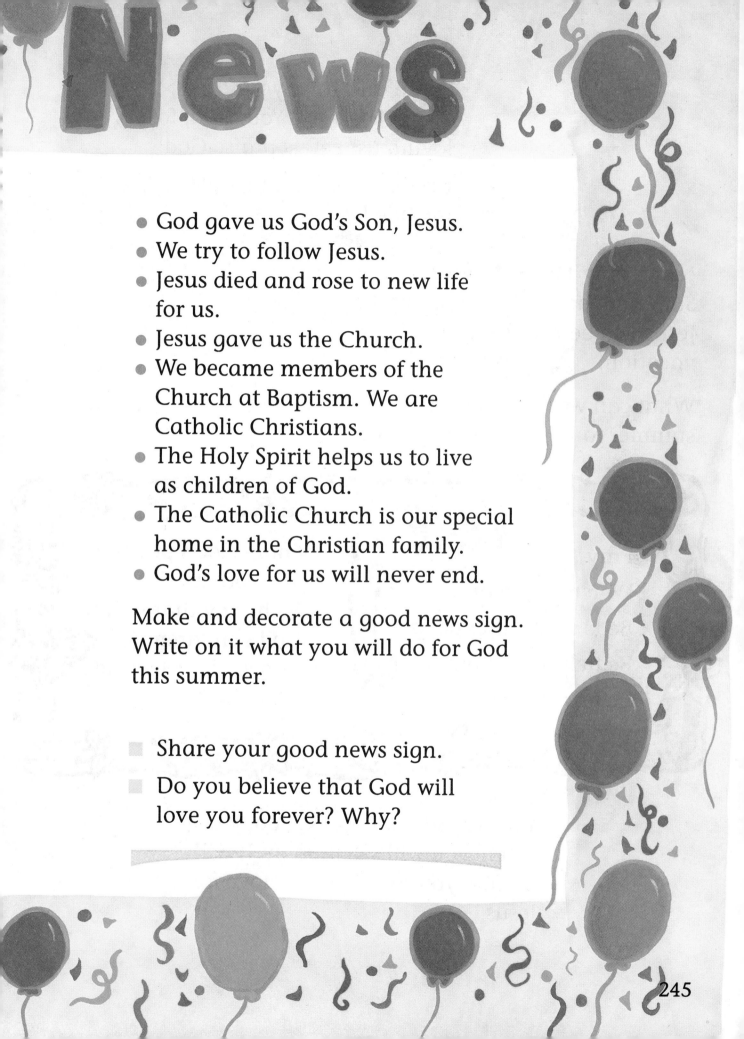

News

- God gave us God's Son, Jesus.
- We try to follow Jesus.
- Jesus died and rose to new life for us.
- Jesus gave us the Church.
- We became members of the Church at Baptism. We are Catholic Christians.
- The Holy Spirit helps us to live as children of God.
- The Catholic Church is our special home in the Christian family.
- God's love for us will never end.

Make and decorate a good news sign. Write on it what you will do for God this summer.

■ Share your good news sign.

■ Do you believe that God will love you forever? Why?

OUR CATHOLIC FAITH

■ Stand and raise your arms. Pray: We praise You, God, for loving us! Let us praise God!

■ How do your summer plans include Jesus?

Jesus Is with Us Always

Summer vacation is coming soon. Jesus will be with us during our vacation.

What can we do during the summer to be a follower of Jesus?

- Pray.
- Worship God at Mass.
- Be kind to other people.
- Be helpful at home.
- Be fair to others.

- Share God's peace with others.
- Be happy that we are God's children.
- Know and celebrate that God loves us.

You can add to this list, too. Place it where you will see it often. It will remind you to show your love for Jesus.

Praise Our Loving God

The Church has a beautiful prayer to praise and honor the Blessed Trinity.

In this prayer, we praise God, who is Father, Son, and Holy Spirit.

Gather in a friendship circle.

Let us end our year together by praising God. We can repeat this prayer until all of us know it well.

† Glory to the Father,
and to the Son,
and to the Holy Spirit
as it was in the beginning,
is now, and will be
for ever. Amen.

Learn by heart **Faith Summary**

- Jesus wants us to be with Him forever.

- God's love will never end.

Coming To Faith

Imagine you are sitting with Jesus.
Talk to Him about what
you have learned.
Tell Him how you will try
to live as a child of God.

I will pray

I will worship God at Mass

I will be kind

I will be fair

Practicing Faith

Mark the pennants to tell
what you will do this summer
to show that you are God's child.

Pray,
† Dear Jesus, help us stay close to you.
Help us to grow as God's children
this summer.

Take a few minutes to talk to the
children about ways they and their
families might use the "Faith Alive"
section. Encourage them to ask
someone at home to do the blessing
prayer with them.

REVIEW ■ TEST

Fill in the circle beside the correct answer.

1. God's love will _____ end.

○ never   ○ always   ○ one day

2. We become members of the Church

at _____ .

○ Baptism   ○ the Eucharist   ○ Confirmation

3. This year we have learned the _____ of Jesus.

○ children   ○ good news   ○ Reconciliation

4. We show we are Jesus' followers when we

are _____ .

○ unkind   ○ unfair   ○ fair

5. How will you live as God's child during vacation?

249

Jesus, give
us peace
in our hearts.

Let us celebrate God's gifts
of forgiveness and peace.
Make a peace pinwheel.

Be still.
Imagine you are the
pinwheel turning.
Pray slowly.

† God's peace . . .
God's peace be in me . . .
God's peace be with us all . . .

Read to me from the Bible

A man who could not walk was carried on a stretcher to see Jesus. Jesus was in someone's house. There was a large crowd around Jesus, so the man's friends lowered him down through the roof.

Jesus said to the man, "Your sins are forgiven. Stand up and go home."

The man began to walk. Everyone was amazed.

From Mark 2:3–12

What do you learn from this story?

Jesus will forgive our sins if we tell Him we are sorry.
Are you sorry for something you have done? Will you tell Jesus?

In this lesson we will discover that peace and forgiveness are gifts from God.

We Will Learn

- We ask Jesus to forgive us.
- God is always ready to forgive us.
- We must be ready to forgive others.

✝ God, may this story help us to remember that You will always love us and are always ready to forgive us. Help us always be ready to forgive one another.

Reader: Once there was a young man who decided to take his father's money and leave his father's home. He went far away, and spent his money on things that were not good for him. When all his money was gone, he had no place to stay and nothing to eat. He knew he had been wrong. He decided to go back home and tell his father how sorry he was.

His father was very happy to see his son once more. He forgave his son and had a party to welcome him home.

From Luke 15:11–24

Leader: Let us use this picture to help us imagine the story Jesus told us about the forgiving father. Think about these questions in your heart:

- How do you think the son feels?
- How do you think the father feels?
- How do you feel when someone who loves you forgives you?

Leader: Now we will say "We are sorry in our hearts." We will ask Jesus to forgive us. We will forgive one another.

Child 1: For the times that we fought with a brother, a sister, or a friend,
All: Jesus, we are sorry.

Child 2: For the times we took something from our friends,
All: Jesus, we are sorry.

Child 3: For the times we disobeyed our parents and did not show respect to older people,
All: Jesus, we are sorry.

Child 4: For the times we did not do the good things we could have done,
All: Jesus, we are sorry.

Child 5: For all the times we have been good and tried to do what You want us to do,
All: Thank You, Jesus!

Turn your pinwheels slowly as you
sing the following song prayer.
(To the tune of "Kumbaya")

♩Give us peace, Jesus, in our hearts. (3x)
O Jesus, give us peace.

Give us peace, Jesus, in our homes. (3x)
O Jesus, give us peace.

Give us peace, Jesus, with our friends. (3x)
O Jesus, give us peace.

Give us peace, Jesus, in our Church. (3x)
O Jesus, give us peace.♩

Now give one another a sign of peace.

Creation is everything made by God.
God made the world and all things in it.
Everything God made is good.
God made all people wonderful.
God wants people to care for all
living things.

God gives you His own life.
Grace is God's own life and
love in you. You can say,
"God is like a loving Parent.
I am God's own child."

God knows and loves us.
There is only one God.
There are three Persons in God:
God the Father, God the Son,
and God the Holy Spirit.
The three Persons in God know
and love us.

God loves and cares for us always.
Sometimes we do what is wrong.
Even then, God loves and cares
for us always.

God gives us Jesus, His
own Son, to show us how to
love God and one another.

Circle **Yes** or **No**.
If you are not sure, circle **?**.

1. Creation is everything made
   by God.   **Yes**   **No**   **?**

2. I am God's own child.   **Yes**   **No**   **?**

3. There are three Persons in one God.   **Yes**   **No**   **?**

4. Grace is another name for
   the Bible.   **Yes**   **No**   **?**

5. Pray the prayer that shows you believe in
   the Blessed Trinity.

Child's name _____

Your child has just completed Unit 1. Have your
child bring this paper to the catechist. It will
help you and the catechist know better how to
help your child grow in the faith.

_____ My child needs help with the part of the
Review I have underlined.

_____ My child understands what has been
taught in this unit.

_____ I would like to speak with you.
My phone number is

_____.

_____
(Signature)

Jesus is part of our human family.
Jesus was human like us.
He laughed and played with His
friends. He loved and cared for
them. At times He was sad or
tired. Jesus did the things we do.

Jesus is God's own Son.
Jesus showed the people how
much God loved them.
Jesus showed by what He did and
said that He was God's own Son.

Jesus is our Friend and Teacher.
Jesus showed the people how
to love and care for one
another. What a happy world
this would be if everyone loved
God, loved all people, and loved
themselves.

Jesus gave Himself for us.
The night before Jesus died He
shared a special meal, the Last
Supper, with His friends. The
next day, Good Friday, Jesus
died for all His friends. On
Easter Sunday, Jesus rose from
the dead to bring us new life.
Jesus is alive and with us today.

Circle the correct answer.

1. Jesus is the —————— of God.

    Father   Son

2. When we talk and listen to God we ——————.

    read   pray

3. Jesus died on ——————.

    Good Friday   Holy Thursday

4. Jesus rose from the dead on ——————.

    Christmas   Easter

5. The prayer Jesus taught is the ——————.

    Our Father   Hail Mary

Child's name _____

Your child has just completed Unit 2. Have your child bring this paper to the catechist. It will help you and the catechist know better how to help your child grow in the faith.

—— My child needs help with the part of the Review I have underlined.

—— My child understands what has been taught in this unit.

—— I would like to speak with you. My phone number is

_____.

_____
(Signature)

God made all things.
God made the world wonderful.
He created plants, animals,
and people. People are special
in God's world. They can know
and love and make things.

God gave people a share in
His own life. This share in
God's life is called grace.

God always loves and cares for us.
He wants us to love and care
for others.

Jesus is God's greatest gift to us.
Jesus is God's own Son.
He shows us how much
God loves us.

Jesus gave us the Law of Love.
He told us to love God, others,
and ourselves. Jesus is our
best friend.

Jesus died on Good Friday and
rose from the dead on Easter
Sunday. He is alive and with
us today.

Circle the correct answer.

1. God _____ to be with us always.

  promises   hopes

2. _____ is God's own Son.

  Jesus   Joseph

3. The _____ is the book of God's story.

  Bible   Reader

4. There are _____ Persons in one God.

  four   three

5. We call God's own life in us _____.

  grace   Mass

6. Tell about one thing you will do to live the Law of Love.

Jesus sends the Holy Spirit.
God the Holy Spirit helped the friends of Jesus to pray and to love others. The Holy Spirit helped them to tell everyone the good news of Jesus

The Church begins.
The Church is Jesus Christ and His baptized friends joined together by the Holy Spirit. The Holy Spirit helps the friends of Jesus to be His Church and to live as Christians.

We celebrate Baptism.
When we are baptized, we become God's own children. We receive God's own life and love. We become part of the Church.

We celebrate Mass.
Mass is our great celebration together. We listen to God's word from the Bible. We receive the Body and Blood of Jesus in Holy Communion.

31 UNIT 3 · TEST

Fill in the circle beside the correct answer.

1. We belong to Jesus' _____.

   ○ room   ○ Church   ○ cross

2. The _____ is with us today.

   ○ friend   ○ Baptism   ○ Holy Spirit

3. We receive _____ in Holy Communion.

   ○ Jesus   ○ water   ○ bread

4. In Baptism I became _____ of God.

   ○ a child   ○ the Person   ○ the Bible

5. Tell how you will love someone as Jesus did.

We belong to a parish.
In our parish we come together
to learn about Jesus and how to
live as Jesus' friends. Everyone
is welcome in our parish family.

We belong to the Catholic Church.
Our Church helps us to be holy
people. We celebrate the sacraments.
In the sacraments our Church does
what Jesus did for His friends.

We learn how to live in our Church.
In our Church we learn how to
be fair to others. Being fair means
treating people the way we want
them to treat us. When we are fair
to one another, we can live in peace.

The Church brings God's forgiveness.
In the Catholic Church we have
a wonderful way to celebrate
that God forgives us. It is called
the sacrament of Reconciliation.
We pray and thank God for
loving us and forgiving us.

God's life lasts forever.
If we live as children of God, we
will be happy with God forever in heaven.

Fill in the circle beside the correct answer.

1. A prayer to the mother of Jesus is the _____.
○ Creed   ○ Hail Mary   ○ Our Father

2. _____ welcomes new members into the Church.
○ Baptism   ○ Eucharist   ○ Reconciliation

3. To worship is to give honor and praise to _____.
○ Mary   ○ Church   ○ God

4. God always forgives us if we are _____.
○ friendly   ○ sorry   ○ old

5. Tell one way you will be a peacemaker.

Jesus Christ sends the Holy Spirit.
The Holy Spirit helps the friends
of Jesus. The Holy Spirit helps
them to be peacemakers.

The Holy Spirit comes to us
when we are baptized.

When we are baptized, we
become part of the Church.

We receive God's own life
and love.

We belong to the Catholic Church.
Everyone is welcome in our
Church. The Church helps us to
be holy people.

We celebrate the sacraments
and try to live fairly and
to be peacemakers.

If we live as children of God, we
will be happy with God forever
in heaven.

33 SECOND SEMESTER ▪ TEST

Fill in the circle beside the correct answer.

1. God sent the _____ to be our Helper.

○ angels   ○ Church   ○ Holy Spirit

2. We belong to the _____ .

○ Holy Family   ○ Church   ○ Blessed Trinity

3. _____ is the good news of Jesus.

○ Baptism   ○ Worship   ○ The gospel

4. Catholics receive the Body and Blood of Jesus
in _____ .

○ Reconciliation   ○ Baptism   ○ Holy Communion

5. Tell one way you will be fair to someone.

The Mass ends.

The priest blesses us.
Then the priest or deacon says,

"Go in peace to love and serve
the Lord."

We answer,
"Thanks be to God."

16

Fold on this line.

My Mass Book

Cut on this line.

Jesus gives us the gift
of Himself in Holy Communion.

14

We ask God to forgive us.

"Lord, have mercy.
Christ, have mercy.
Lord, have mercy."

After a prayer, we
sit and get ready to
hear God's word.

3

We gather as a parish family.
We stand and pray.

✝ In the name of the Father,
and of the Son,
and of the Holy Spirit.
We answer,
"Amen."

Cut on this line.

Communion time is a
wonderful time for us
to pray.

You can say,
✝ "Jesus, come and live
in my heart."

Fold on this line.

Liturgy of the Word

We listen to God's word.
The reader says,
"The word of the Lord."

We answer,
"Thanks be
to God."

We share the gift of peace.
We say,
"Peace be with you."

We stand and pray the prayer
Jesus taught us.

† "Our Father, who art in heaven,
hallowed be thy name;
thy kingdom come;
thy will be done on earth
as it is in heaven.
Give us this day our daily bread;
and forgive us our trespasses
as we forgive those
who trespass against us;
and lead us not into temptation,
but deliver us from evil."

Cut on this line.

We stand for the gospel.
The priest or deacon says,
"The Lord be with you."

We answer,
"And also with you."

After the gospel, the priest or
deacon says,
"The gospel of the Lord."

We say,
"Praise to you, Lord Jesus Christ."

"This is the cup of my blood."

The priest invites us to pray.
He says,
"Lift up your hearts."

We answer,
"We lift them up to the Lord."

Liturgy of the Eucharist

Our gifts of bread and wine are carried to the altar.

The priest prepares our gifts to be offered to God.

Cut on this line.

We pray,
"Holy,
   holy,
     holy
Lord, God of power and might...."

"Do this in memory of me."

We remember what Jesus said and did at the Last Supper.

The priest does what Jesus did at the Last Supper and says,

"This is my body which will be given up for you."

My Catholic Faith Book

For the Family

As your child's first grade experience ends, we celebrate with you the ways in which your child has grown as a child of God. You have guided your child's growth in the wisdom of Christian faith, including a love for Scripture. During this year, your child has learned and experienced some very important truths of our faith as they are contained in the *Catechism of the Catholic Church*. For example:

- **Creed:** God gave us His Son, Jesus Christ. We are members of God's family, the Church. The Holy Spirit helps us to live as children of God.

- **Sacraments:** We become members of the Church at Baptism. We thank Jesus at Mass for the gift of Himself in the Eucharist. In the sacrament of Reconciliation, we celebrate God's forgiveness. We are strengthened by the Holy Spirit at Confirmation.

- **Morality:** We try to follow Jesus. We try to love God, one another, and ourselves. We try to be fair and to live in peace.

- **Prayer:** We listen to God's word in the Bible. We talk to God in our own words. We pray the Our Father, the Hail Mary, and the Sign of the Cross.

Continue to encourage your child to grow in faith by going to Mass together, singing the faith songs, reading Bible stories about God's love for us, and praying together.

Family Prayer

Dear God,
Help our family to continue to grow in faith each day. God, help us as we grow more like Jesus Christ, Your Son. Amen.

This is what we believe…

God made the world and all people.
Everything God made is good.
He made us and loves us.

He knows and loves and creates.
God made us to know and love
and make things.

There is only one God.
There are three Persons in one God:
God the Father, God the Son, and
God the Holy Spirit.

We call the three Persons in God
the Blessed Trinity.
God's love for us will never end.

C
R
E
E
D

This is how we pray…

We can pray anywhere or anytime
by ourselves or with others.

We listen to God's word in the Bible.

We talk to God in our own words
or say special prayers we have
learned, the Sign of the Cross,
the Our Father, and the Hail Mary.
We begin to learn the Apostles' Creed.

We praise God, thank Him,
or ask Him for help.
We tell God we are sorry
if we have hurt Him
or other people.

P
R
A
Y
E
R

Jesus is God's greatest gift to us. Jesus is God's own Son. He shows us how much God loves us.

Jesus gave us the Law of Love. He told us to love God, others, and ourselves.

Jesus died on Good Friday and rose from the dead on Easter Sunday. He is alive and with us today. Jesus gives us new life.

Jesus gave us the Church.

This is how we live...

We try to follow Jesus.

M   We try to follow the Law of Love.

O   We love God, others, and ourselves.

R   We care for God's world.

A   We care for all people.

L   We care especially for the poor and needy.

I   We try to live fairly.

T   We try to be peacemakers.

Y

The Church is the community of Jesus' baptized friends.

We are joined together by the Holy Spirit. The Holy Spirit helps the friends of Jesus to be His Church.

We became members of the Church at Baptism. We are Catholic Christians.

At Baptism, we receive God's own life and love. We call this grace.

The Catholic Church is our special home in the Christian family.

The Holy Spirit helps us live as children of God.

We can live forever in heaven with God.

This is how we celebrate…

S — We celebrate the sacrament of Baptism. When we are baptized, we receive God's own life and love.

A — In the sacrament of Confirmation we receive the gift of the Holy Spirit in a special way.

C — We celebrate the Mass. We hear God's word and share the Body and Blood of Christ.

R —

A — We celebrate the sacrament of Eucharist at Mass. We share Jesus' gift of Himself in Holy Communion.

M —

E — We celebrate the sacrament of Reconciliation. We tell God we are sorry and we celebrate that God is always ready to forgive us.

N

T

S

Morning Offering

My God, I offer you today
all I think and do and say,
uniting it with what was done
on earth, by Jesus Christ,
your Son.

Evening Prayer

Dear God, before I sleep
I want to thank you
for this day so full of
your kindness and your joy.
I close my eyes to rest
safe in your loving care.

FOLD

My Prayer Screen

FOLD

A Listening Prayer

God, open our ears
and hearts to listen
to your word.

From Psalm 27:11

Prayers from the Bible

God,
teach me to do
what you want.
Please show me
the way.

From Psalm 27:11

God,
I am always
in your care.

From Psalm 31:15

Grace Before Meals

Bless us, O Lord,
and these your gifts,
which we are about to receive
from your bounty,
through Christ our Lord.
Amen.

Grace After Meals

We give you thanks,
almighty God,
for these and all your gifts
which we have received
through Christ our Lord.
Amen.

FOLD

FOLD

GLUE

GLUE

Prayer of Quiet

Sit in a comfortable position.
Relax by breathing in and out.
Shut out all the sights
and sounds.
Each time you breathe in
and out, say the name "Jesus."

Prayer for Peace

Give us peace, Jesus,
in our hearts.
Give us peace, Jesus,
in our homes.
Give us peace, Jesus,
with our friends.
Give us peace, Jesus,
in our Church.
O, Jesus, give us peace.

Family Prayer

Come, Holy Spirit,
fill our hearts
with love.

Holy Family,
help our family
to be a
holy family, too.

A Family Blessing

May God bless us and
take care of us.
May God be kind to us.
May He look on us
with favor.
May He give us peace,
every season, every year.

From Numbers 6:24–26

GLUE

back of screen 2

GLUE

FOLD

FOLD

GLUE

Prayers
for Church Seasons

Advent

Come, Lord Jesus.

Christmas

Jesus, we welcome you
into our hearts.

Lent

Jesus, help me spend
quiet time with you.

Easter

Alleluia, Jesus!
We have good news
to tell.

Ordinary Time

Jesus, may our friendship
with you keep on growing.

Hail Mary

Hail Mary, full of grace,
the Lord is with you;
blessed are you
among women,
and blessed is the fruit
of your womb, Jesus.
Holy Mary, Mother of God,
pray for us sinners
now and at the hour
of our death.
Amen.

I Believe

I believe in God,
the Father almighty,
creator of heaven and earth.

The rest of the Apostles' Creed
will be taught in Grades 2 and 3.

— FOLD —

Sign of the Cross

In the name of the Father,
and of the Son,
and of the Holy Spirit.
Amen.

Our Father

Our Father, who art in heaven,
hallowed be thy name;
thy kingdom come;
thy will be done on earth
as it is in heaven.
Give us this day our daily bread
and forgive us our trespasses
as we forgive those
who trespass against us;
and lead us not into temptation
but deliver us from evil.
Amen.

— FOLD —

Glory to the Father

Glory to the Father,
and to the Son,
and to the Holy Spirit
as it was in the beginning,
is now, and will be forever.
Amen.

A Vocation Prayer

God, I know you will
call me for special work
in my life. Help me
to follow Jesus each day
and be ready to answer
your call.

We honor Mary, the mother of Jesus, God's own Son.

We use statues and pictures to help us remember:
• Mary cared for Jesus.
• She is our mother, too.

Mary's special month is May.

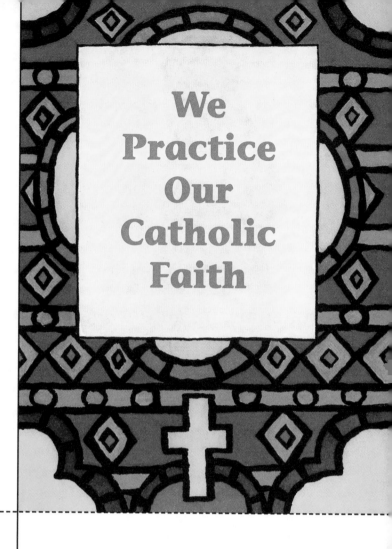

We Practice Our Catholic Faith

We pray to God at home by ourselves or with our families.
We pray to God in church with our parish family.

Fold on this line.

We are baptized.
We are God's children.
We use holy water as a sign of our Baptism.

We often begin our prayers with the sign of the cross. Bless yourself by making the sign of the cross with your right hand.

Fold on this line.

We celebrate special days called holy days.

- The Immaculate Conception (December 8)

- Christmas (December 25)

- Mary, Mother of God (January 1)

- Ascension Thursday (40 days after Easter)

- Assumption of Mary (August 15)

- All Saints' Day (November 1)

Cut on this line.

Mass is our great celebration together.
We take part in the Mass on Sunday or on Saturday evening.

We show respect and love for God in church. Genuflect by bending your right knee to the floor.

Saint Joseph

Saint Elizabeth

Saint Thérèse

Saint Martin de Porres

Saint Nicholas

Saint Joseph,
you cared for Jesus and
Mary. You worked with your
hands. Help us to use our
hands to show love and
care for our family.

Saint Thérèse,
you prayed for people to
help them get to know Jesus.
Help us remember to pray
for our families, friends, and
all in need.

Saint Elizabeth,
you helped the poor and
hungry. Show us ways to
help all who are poor,
as you did.

Saint Martin de Porres,
you helped the poor, the sick,
and the homeless. Help us to
love and care for someone
who is sick.

Saint _____,
pray for us.

Saint Nicholas,
you were a special friend to
poor children. Help us to
share what we have with
those who have less.

CLOSING PRAYER SERVICE

Leader: See how the Father has loved us! God's love is so great that we are called God's children.

From 1 John 3:1

Dear God, we are Your children. We thank You for all Your gifts.

Reader: For making us. . .
All: Thank You, God!

Reader: For loving us. . .
All: Thank You, God!

Reader: For never leaving us. . .
All: Thank You, God!

Reader: For the Holy Spirit. . .
All: Thank You, God!

Reader: For giving us Jesus. . .
All: Thank You, God!

Draw a picture of one of your gifts from God.

At the top of your picture write:

Thank You, God, for the gift of

_____.

Carry your picture in procession. Sing this song.

♫ Let us pray and celebrate, Alleluia, Gifts and signs of God's great love, Alleluia. ♫

(To the tune of "Michael, Row the Boat")

GLOSSARY

Advent (page 128)
The name Christians give to our waiting time before we celebrate Jesus' birth at Christmas. We continue to wait until Jesus comes again.

Baptism (page 161)
The sacrament that gives us a share in God's life and makes us His own children and members of Jesus' Church.

Bible (page 66)
The book that tells God's story.

Blessed Trinity (page 47)
The three Persons in one God: the Father, the Son, and the Holy Spirit.

Catholic Church (page 153)
The baptized followers of Jesus who are joined together by the Holy Spirit under the leadership of the pope and bishops.

Christians (page 150)
Followers of Jesus Christ.

Christmas Day (page 79)
The day we celebrate the birth of Jesus.

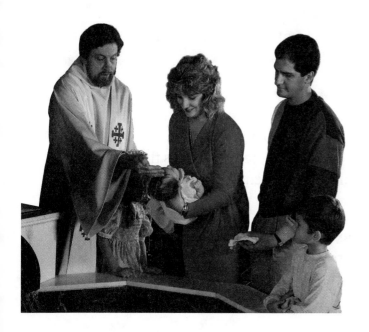

Confirmation (page 214)
The sacrament in which the Holy Spirit comes to us in a special way.

Creation (page 20)
Everything made by God.

Easter Sunday (page 121)
The day Jesus rose from the dead.

Eucharist (page 215)
The sacrament in which we receive the Body and Blood of Christ.

Good Friday (page 120)
The day Jesus died on the cross for all people.

Gospel (page 181)
The good news that God loves us and gives us Jesus Christ, the Son of God.

Grace (page 39)
God's own life and love in us.

Holy Communion (page 119)
The Body and Blood of Christ.

Holy Family (page 80)
The family of Jesus, Mary, and Joseph.

Holy Spirit (page 141)
The third Person of the Blessed Trinity, the Helper sent to us by Jesus.

Jesus Christ (page 78)
The Son of God and the Son of Mary.

Last Supper (page 118)
The last meal Jesus had with His friends before He died. At this meal, Jesus gave us the gift of the Eucharist.

Law of Love (page 111)
Jesus teaches us to love God and others as we love ourselves.

Lent (page 190)
Lent is the special time before Easter. We pray and try to grow as followers of Jesus.

Mary (page 78)
Mary is the mother of Jesus, God's own Son. Mary is our mother too.

Mass (page 171)
The special celebration in which we hear God's word, remember Jesus dying and rising, and share the Body and Blood of Christ.

Parish (page 203)
The special place where Jesus' friends come together to pray.

Pope (page 154)
The pope is the leader of the Catholic Church.

Prayer (page 101)
Talking and listening to God.

Reconciliation (page 215)
The sacrament in which the Church brings us God's forgiveness and mercy.

Sacraments (page 214)
Signs through which Jesus shares God's own life and love with us.

Saints (page 72)
People who loved God very much, and who are now happy with God forever in heaven.

Sin (page 232)
The act of freely choosing to do what we know to be wrong. We disobey God's law on purpose.

Worship (page 215)
Giving honor and praise to God.

Acknowledgments

Grateful acknowledgment is due the following for their work on the *Coming to Faith Program*.

Patricia Dobrowski, Project Director
Angela Dinger, Editor
Tresse De Lorenzo, Manager: Production/Art
Joe Svadlenka, Art Director
Stuart Vance, Manager: Electronic Art/Production
Walter Norfleet, Design Director
Jeanne Whitney, Designer

Excerpts and adaptations from *Good News Bible*, copyright © American Bible Society 1966, 1971, 1976, 1979.

Excerpts from the English translation of *Rite of Baptism for Children* © 1969, International Committee on English in the Liturgy, Inc. (ICEL); excerpts from the English translation of *The Roman Missal* © 1973, ICEL. All rights reserved.

English translation of the Lord's Prayer by the International Consultation on English Texts.

Photo Research
Jim Saylor

Cover Photos
Peter Brandt : *background and nature insets.*
Myrleen Cate : *top right insets.*
CNS/ CROSIERS : *bottom left insets.*

Photo Credits
Diane Ali : 66, 197 *bottom left.*
Jeffrey Aranita : 158.
Myrleen Cate: 32, 35 *bottom,* 40, 42, 46–47, 48, 48/49, 51 *top,* 52, 76 *center,* 76 *bottom,* 93, 96, 104, 106, 107, 124, 128, 129, 152, 178, 186, 189, 192, 197 *bottom right,* 198, 207 *top,* 207 *center,* 218 *bottom right,* 222 *top,* 223, 226, 228, 240, 250, 254.
CROSIERS/ Gene Plaisted, OSC: 207 *bottom left.*
Michael Krasowitz/ FPG International: 82 *top.*
Kathy Ferguson: 28 *bottom,* 29, 41 *right,* 56/57, 97, 113, 203, 217.
Chip Henderson/ Picturesque: 222 *bottom.*
Ken Karp: 155, 241, 247.
Ron Kimball: 35 *center.*
Jeane Claude Francolon/ LIAISON International: 49.
MARYKNOLL/ Frank Breen, MM: 213 *top;* J. Padula: 212/213.
H. Armstrong Roberts: 18 *left,* 34, 41 *left,* 194, 197 *top.*
James Shaffer: 51 *bottom,* 212, 213 *bottom.*
Howard E. Simmons: 218 *top.*
Nancy Sheehan: 3, 11 *bottom,* 12, 102, 110, 154, 162/163, 164, 204, 205, 218 *bottom left.*
The Stock Market/ Ariel Skelley: 35 *top;* Nancy Brown: 92; Henley & Savage: 153.
Ken Krakow/ The Stock Source-Atlanta: 202.
Tony Stone Images/ Art Wolfe: 18 *right;* David Higgs: 18 *bottom;* Mitch Reardon: 19 *left;* TSI: 19 *right;* David Young-Wolff: 28 *top.* Andy Sacks: 50.
Tom McCarthy/ Transparencies, Inc: 83.
Jim Whitmer: 10 *right,* 10 *left,* 175, 179, 206, 216.

Illustrators
Blaine Martin: Cover, Digital Imaging

Angela Adams: 114, 208B, 228.
David Barnett: 66-67.
Marilyn Barr: 22, 76, 77, 84, 148, 168, 188, 189, 200-201, 208A.
Andrea Barrett: 159, 247, 267, 279.
Shirley Beckes: 136, 222-223.
Teresa Berasi: 93.
Greta Buchart: 27, 227, 233.
Janice Castiglione: 44.
Antonio Castro: 90-91.
Eulala Conner: 132, 133, 140-141, 238, 242-243.
Gwen Connoly: 128-129.
Renee Daily: 122-123, 183, 184.
Len Ebert: 281.
Allan Eitzen: 16-17.
Adam Gordon: 162, 163, 216.
Megan Halsey: 244-245.
Brad Hamann: 29, 99, 111, 206.
John Haysom: 100-101, 170-171.
Ronda Henrichsen: 146, 210-211, 248, 250, 254.
Sunshine De La Rosa Jouvin: 62.
Laura Kelly: 108-109.
Anne Kennedy: 275.
Elliot Kreloff: 166.
Dora Leder: 24, 25, 30, 31, 36-37, 70-71, 103.
Susan Lexa: 9, 38-39, 68, 74, 94, 145, 210, 237.
Diana Magnuson: 14, 15, 45, 64, 72-73, 86, 87, 116-117, 134-135, 169, 180-181, 224-225.
Shelly Matheis: 160-161.
Anni Matsick: 13, 26, 27, 54, 55, 138, 139.
Marty Norman: 65.
Olivia: 165, 185.
Debra Page-Trim: 71.
Debra Pickney: 87, 236.
Lainé Roundy: 10-11, 56-57, 92, 174, 182-183, 195, 196-197.
Margaret Sanfilippo: 21, 58-59, 60-61, 78-79, 80-81, 142-143, 144, 174, 182, 232-233, 236, 252-253.
Bob Shein: 107.
Tom Sperling: 88-89, 120-121, 150-151, 190-191, 214-215, 234-235, 251.
Sally Springer: 149.
Matt Straub: 246.
Susan Swan: 179, 202-203, 231.
Peggy Tagel: 40, 152-153.
Nancy Tobin: 212-213.
Stan Tusan: 176, 178, 186, 240, 241.
Jenny Vainisi: 112.
David Wenzel: 98-99, 118-119.
Jenny Williams: 126, 127, 130, 156, 220, 221, 230.
Elizabeth Wolf: 20.